THE MOUNTAIN ENVIRONMENT

SCHOOLS ABROAD

Chancerel

Other books available from Schools Abroad:

In France

In France Workbook (September 1984)

Passeport pour la France

In Germany

In Switzerland

Classical and Modern Greece

Italy down the Ages

Learning to Ski

The way to play Soccer

The Mediterranean Port/Nautical Guide

The Neptunia Project Book

The Mediterranean Environment (March 1985)

Photographs

Heather Angel – 39

Association Suisse pour L'Equipement Technique de l'Agriculture – 45, 46

Audisio – 53(4), 55

Aerofilms Ltd. – 7, 19, 93

Associated Press – 81

Austrian State Tourist Office – 32, 58, 64, 71, 94

Mary Briggs – 34, 35(5)

British Columbia Government – 67

British Tourist Authority – 7

Bibliothèque Forney, Paris – 55

Bulgarian Tourist Board – 90

Canada National Film Board – 66(2)

Canadian High Commission – 37, 67(2)

Civil Aviation Authority – 74(3), 75(2)

Bruce Coleman Ltd./Hans Reinhard – 39

Cogefar s.p.a., Milan – 73

Daily Telegraph/Anthony Howarth – 43

C. M. Dixon – 16

DP – 5, 19, 37, 47, 66, 67, 71

Durst – 92

EDF Photothèque, Paris – 6, 64

Mary Evans Picture Library – 72, 79, 80, 81

Finnish Tourist Office – 18

Foto E.P.T., Turin – 56

French Government Tourist Office – 38, 44, 54, 59(2), 87

Geoscience Features – 47

Habeggar SA/H Heiniger Spiez – 71

Prof. Haimendorf/School of Oriental Studies – 42, 43(2)

Italian State Tourist Office (ENIT) – 5, 24, 54, 57(2), 63

Institute of Geological Sciences – 4, 11, 21

John Massey Stewart – 78

Meteorological Office – 29(4)

Ministry of Defence – 32

Musées Nationaux, Paris – 81

Musée Regionale de l'Auvergne – 53

National Portrait Gallery – 82(2)

Norway Travel Association – 25

Norwegian Tourist Office – 4

Office du Tourisme, Chamonix – 55

OPAV, Valais, Switzerland – 4, 46(2)

Photopress Grenoble/Rhône Poulenc SA – 65

Phototheque Gendarmerie Nationale, Paris – 33(2)

SA des Eaux Minerales D'Evian – 59, 62(2)

Service des Avalanches Suisse – 26, 27(3)

Servicio Aero-fotographico Nacional, Peru/Frank W. Lane – 21

Solarfilm, Iceland – 7(2)

Swiss National Tourist Office – 3(2), 17(2), 20, 25(2), 39, 45(3), 46(2), 53, 59(3), 63(3), 71(2), 72, 73(2), 79, 83(2), 88(2), 89(2)

Tate Gallery – 83

TI Raleigh Ltd. – 86

W. A. Bentley and W. J. Humphreys – 24(3), 25

Yugoslavian Tourist Office – 79, 91

Every effort has been made to trace and acknowledge every photograph used.

ISBN 0-905703-59-6

© Twinburn Limited/Schools Abroad 1980

Second Edition 1981

Reprinted 1984

Chancerel Publishers Ltd.,
40 Tavistock Street,
London WC2E 7PB.

Schools Abroad Group,
Grosvenor Hall,
Bolnore Road,
Haywards Heath,
West Sussex RH16 4BX.

Produced by Chancerel Publishers Ltd.
Graphic reproduction by ReproSharp Ltd.. London
Printed by OFSA, Milan.

The publishers would like to acknowledge the assistance of the following in the preparation of the revised edition of this book: A. Audisio; M. Briggs; M. Contri (Assessorato al Turismo, Turin); A. Goudie; J. Harries (project illustrations); G. Levitt; D. Lock (cartoon page 41); S. Thomas.

Cover: The front cover of this book shows the Aletschwald Nature Reserve and the Aletsch Glacier in Switzerland. On the back cover there is a Swiss Federal Topographic Service map of the same area.

"Le attività di carattere educativo sono finalizzate a diffondere, in particolare tra la popolazione scolastica e giovanile, la conoscenza e il respetto della montagna e dei suoi valori ambientali e culturali, nonché la conoscenza delle nozioni relative alla sicurezza del turista."

Legge regionale 30 Maggio, 1980,
Regione Piemonte.

THE MOUNTAIN ENVIRONMENT

Edited by
Duncan Prowse

Contributors and consultants
Andrew Goudie, MA, PhD, Professor of Geography, Oxford University,
Fellow of Hertford College, Oxford.
Greg Levitt, BSc, Cert Ed, Headmaster, Aylesford School, Maidstone, Kent.
Spencer Thomas, BA, PhD, Head of Geography at West Sussex Institute of Higher
Education.
Mary Briggs, FPS, FLS, Hon. General Secretary of the Botanical Society
of the British Isles.
Andrew Jennings, MA, FIFor, Director, Economic Forestry Group.
John Kirkaldy, MSc (Econ), Dip Ed, PhD, Lecturer in Modern History at the Open
University and North London Polytechnic.
G. Raniero, Assessorato alla Montagna, Regione Piemonte, Turin, Italy.
Aldo Audisio, Direttore Tecnico, Museo Nazionale della Montagna Duca Degli
Abruzzi, Turin, Italy.

Research by
Ruth Thomson
Paul Dosaj
Susie Bricknell (Paris)
Florence Grommier (Turin)

Designed by
Valerie Sargent

Project Development Manager for Schools Abroad
Barbara Hopper

SCHOOLS ABROAD

Chancerel

Contents

Folded strata

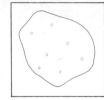

Snow flakes

Glaciated fjord, Norway

Sion Valley, Switzerland

Swiss chalet

Hydro electric turbine

Traditional costume

The Dolomites, Italy

Mountain road, Japan

I. The Mountains of the world

Our planet earth is quite unimaginably old. It dates back about 4,500 million years, and throughout that time it has been changing constantly. Some 200 million years ago, all the continents were joined in one giant land mass. In 150 million years' time Africa and Europe will overlap, obliterating the Mediterranean, while Australia will have almost filled the gap between North America and Japan. At times there have been vast ice sheets covering much of the earth, volcanoes have erupted into high mountains, rifts have appeared, oceans opened and chains of mountains piled up.

Old and new mountains

The world has never been without mountain building movements, and the results of many of them are still with us. Greenland, at the age of about 3,800 million years, is one of the oldest mountain areas.

The Alps and the Himalayas are relatively young at a mere 25 million years old. Some mountains are still being built, rising at rates of about 13m (43ft) every 1,000 years, which is faster than erosion can wear them down.

Other mountains, like those in Scotland, have been worn away to stubs. Soon (in geological terms) they will be hills only. Geologists reckon that at least 700m (2,300ft) of steep hillside is needed to qualify as a mountain.

Five types of mountain

The world has various types of mountains. There are the **volcanoes**, which may stand in solitary peaks, like Mt Etna, or in clusters, like the islands of Indonesia or Japan.

There are **block mountains**, like Mt Ruwenzori, left standing at over 5,000m (16,500ft) while the ground around it dropped away to form the East African Rift Valley.

There are the ancient **shield mountains** of Scotland, Scandinavia and Labrador, whose origins and shape have long ago been obscured by millions of years of erosion.

There are the **undersea mountains**, which are the greatest of all. One chain, the Mid-Atlantic Ridge, starts north of Iceland, runs the whole length of the Atlantic ocean, and round into the Indian Ocean, a distance of about 40,000km (25,000 miles). Other underwater mountain ranges run round the Pacific Ocean, and round Antarctica, south of Australia. Some of the mountains in the sea would dwarf Everest.

The largest and most famous chains of mountains in the world are **fold mountains** – the youngest, highest and most jagged of all. They are arranged in two great belts around the

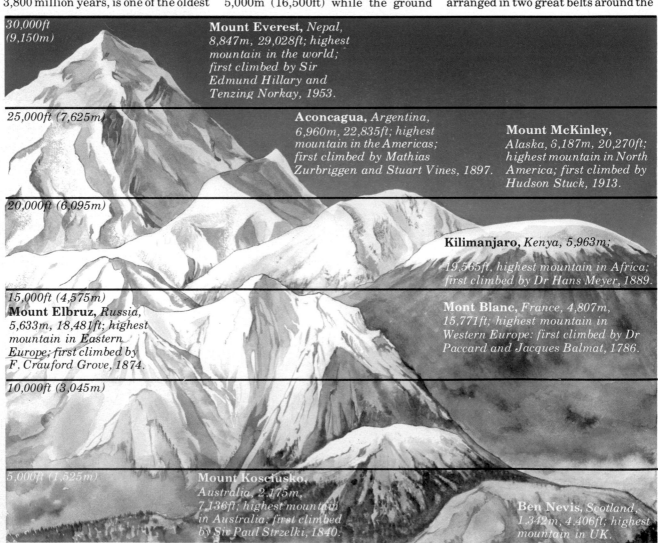

30,000ft (9,150m)

Mount Everest, *Nepal, 8,847m, 29,028ft; highest mountain in the world; first climbed by Sir Edmund Hillary and Tenzing Norkay, 1953.*

25,000ft (7,625m)

Aconcagua, *Argentina, 6,960m, 22,835ft; highest mountain in the Americas; first climbed by Mathias Zurbriggen and Stuart Vines, 1897.*

Mount McKinley, *Alaska, 6,187m, 20,270ft; highest mountain in North America; first climbed by Hudson Stuck, 1913.*

20,000ft (6,095m)

Kilimanjaro, *Kenya, 5,963m; 19,565ft, highest mountain in Africa; first climbed by Dr Hans Meyer, 1889.*

15,000ft (4,575m)

Mount Elbruz, *Russia, 5,633m, 18,481ft; highest mountain in Eastern Europe; first climbed by F. Crauford Grove, 1874.*

Mont Blanc, *France, 4,807m, 15,771ft; highest mountain in Western Europe; first climbed by Dr Paccard and Jacques Balmat, 1786.*

10,000ft (3,045m)

5,000ft (1,525m)

Mount Kosciusko, *Australia, 2,175m, 7,136ft; highest mountain in Australia; first climbed by Sir Paul Strzelki, 1840.*

Ben Nevis, *Scotland, 1,342m, 4,406ft; highest mountain in UK.*

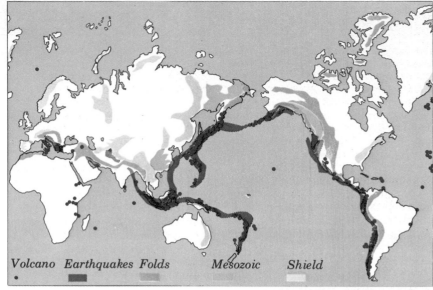

earth.

One runs longitudinally, from the Pyrenees between France and Spain, through the Alps in France, Switzerland and Austria, through Bulgaria, Turkey, Iran, Afghanistan to the Himalayas of Nepal and Tibet. There are relatively few volcanoes in these mountains. But the other system is known as the **Ring of Fire**, because it has so many of them.

The fold mountains and active volcanoes of the Ring of Fire surround the Pacific Ocean. They include ranges like the Rockies, with Mt Saint Helens, which erupted spectacularly in 1980, the Andes, with Volcan Cayambe, at 5,795m (19,014ft) the highest point on the Equator, the Southern Alps of New Zealand, the mountains of the Philippines, Japan and the Aleutian Islands of Alaska. Most of the world's earthquakes and eruptions take place in these regions.

Volcano Earthquakes Folds   Mesozoic   Shield

Above: *The world's highest mountains are the youngest, arranged in two chains, one from the Pyrenees to the Himalayas, one round the Pacific, the 'Ring of Fire'.*

Above left: *The eroded folds of Mount Everest.* **Above:** *A rounded ancient shield mountain, Ben Nevis, Scotland.* **Above right:** *Surtsey, a new volcano emerges off Iceland, Nov. 1963.* **Right:** *Six months later Surtsey has become an island. Lava still flows from the crater into the sea.*

How mountains are made

The familiar steep and jagged peaks of mountains are mostly caused by forces that destroy. Glaciers, rivers, frost and even men wear away mountains constantly. But all the forces that erode mountains are nothing compared to those that build them.

It is only in the last twenty years that scientists have begun to make sense of the way in which the world's mountains and continents are formed. Long ago people noticed that the coasts of Africa and South America seemed to fit together. But it was not until 1912 that the German Alfred Wegener put forward his theory of **continental drift**. It is only since the 1960's that the current theory of **plate tectonics** has been added to it.

Plate tectonics

Below the earth's crust is a **mantle** of **magma** – a deep layer of semi-molten rock. This is kept extremely hot by radioactivity. Some of the heat escapes through the crust, like warmth from a household radiator. But for the rest, safety valves are needed so that some of the magma can escape. These are the volcanoes and under-sea lava flows.

The surface crust of the earth is divided into several rigid **plates**, part continental land, part sea-bed. Each plate floats on magma. Once, all the plates were placed in such a way that the continents made up a single mass of land, called Pangaea. Wegener tried to prove this by finding identical fossils and rock structures in South America and Africa.

The rest of the globe was covered by water, much as today 70 per cent of the world is covered by sea.

Continental drift

Since that time, 200 million years ago, the continents have been drifting slowly, at a rate that would close the Straits of Dover in a million years.

As a plate moves, it collides with some of its neighbours and pulls away from others. In the centre of each of the oceans is a mountain ridge. It is here that the plates are pulled apart. Magma forces its way up between the plates, solidifying and filling the gaps.

When one plate pushes against another several things happen. Rocks on the edge of one plate are **folded** and **twisted**, like the front of a car in a crash. One of the plates slides under the other, **uplifting** the top one high above its previous level. In this way the Alps were formed by the African Plate moving north, and the Andes were pushed up by the Pacific Nazca

Right: *200 million years ago all the continents were joined in one land mass. Since then the continents have been drifting apart. South America and Africa used to be joined, as can be seen from their similar coasts.*

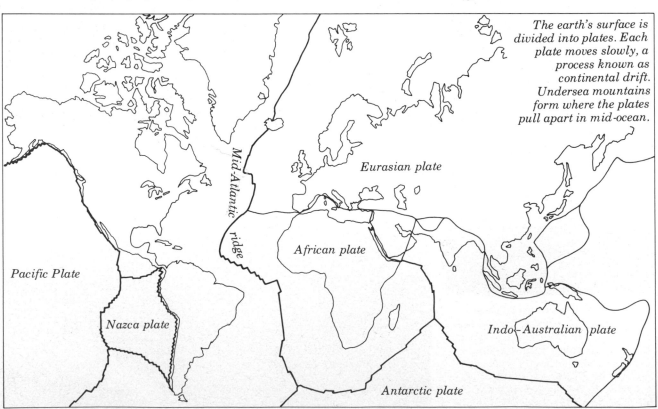

The earth's surface is divided into plates. Each plate moves slowly, a process known as continental drift. Undersea mountains form where the plates pull apart in mid-ocean.

Mid-Atlantic ridge

Eurasian plate

African plate

Pacific Plate

Nazca plate

Indo-Australian plate

Antarctic plate

Plate colliding with the South American continent.

The forces unleashed by such a collision are tremendous. Great cracks appear in the newly folded and twisted mountains, causing earthquakes. Magma escapes through the cracks, erupting through volcanoes. The lower plate is pushed down into the earth, making an **ocean trench**, like the Marianas Trench off the Philippines, deepest in the world at 11,022m (36,372ft). The part of the earth's crust that was the ocean floor plunges down to be reabsorbed into the hot mantle.

There is thus a constant cycle, with one edge of the plate being added to in mid-ocean, and the other edge being eaten away under the next door plate. The life expectancy of any piece of ocean floor is only about 200 million years.

This process, however, does not work so well when two continents, at the leading edges of their respective plates, meet head on. The surface crust of continents is very thick – 60km (37.5 miles) under the Alps. This does not melt easily into the mantle, but instead pushes the mountains higher, crumpling them to extremes. This has already happened with the closing of the sea between India and the Himalayas, and will happen again as Africa moves north, closing up the Mediterranean.

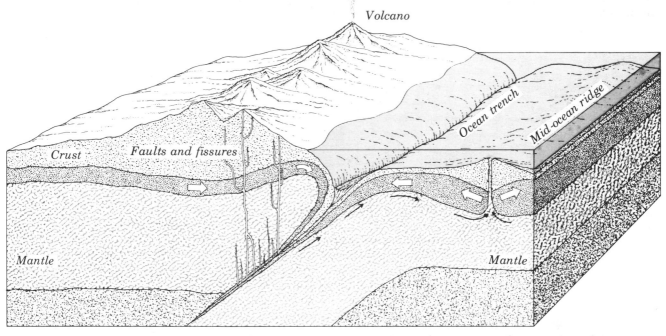

Below: *Cross section of a typical plate, consisting partly of continental land mass and partly of sea bed. The leading edge of the plate, where it collides with the next plate, is folded and uplifted, resulting in jagged mountains. The trailing edge is continually being added on to by outflows of magma in mid-ocean.*

Above: *Where plates collide the crust of one is forced down underneath the other, forming a deep ocean trench. By contrast the upper plate is buckled and lifted forming mountains. Rocks crack, causing earthquakes. Volcanoes erupt through fissures.*

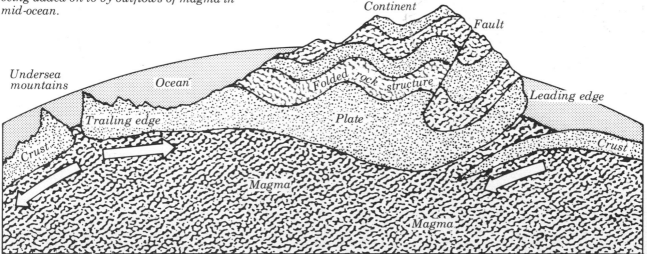

Rocks and fossils

When a volcano erupts it shows us the beginning of the processes that construct all the world's rocks. The raw material is magma from the mantle. The natural stresses and strains of the earth do the rest, forging it into one of three basic types of rock.

Three kinds of rocks

Igneous rocks are the closest relations of magma. They make up about 75 per cent of the earth's crust. They are either blasted to the surface through volcanoes, or forced up between other layers of rock below ground. Later, softer surrounding rocks are eroded, leaving only outcrops, like the granite tors of Dartmoor.

Igneous rocks, that flow easily to the surface through the thin crust below the sea, cool quickly and remain very similar to the basic magma. Basalt is one of the commonest of these. Other igneous rocks mix with the melting underside of a continent into a thick lava that cools slowly as it rises to make granite, the foundation rock of continents.

Once new rocks reach the surface they are attacked by all the agents of erosion. Glaciers, weather, even plants and people, constantly chip pieces off the mountains and rivers carry the debris to the sea. There the river deposits layer after layer of sediment, sometimes building a huge delta at the mouth, like the Nile or the Ganges.

The result is that although **sedimentary rocks** only make up five per cent of the world's total, they are the commonest surface rocks, acting like a thin skin about 2.5km (1.6 miles) deep over much of the earth.

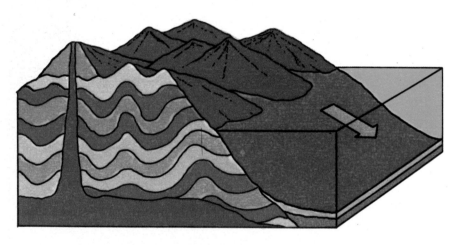

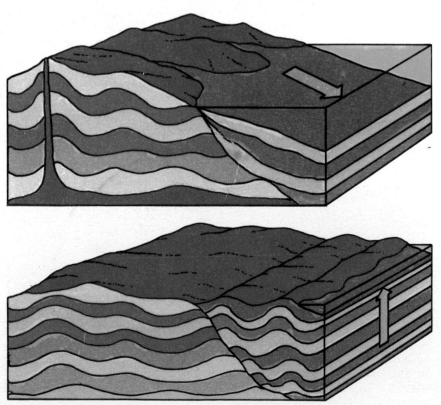

Left: *The process by which sedimentary rocks are formed.*

Top: *Mountain building movements push up high ranges.*

Centre: *All the agents of erosion, water, frost, wind, break down the hills, and rivers carry the debris to the sea, where it is laid down in layers.*

Bottom: *New movements of the earth's crust uplift the layers of sedimentary rock. Under great heat or pressure sedimentary rocks are changed into metamorphic rocks. For example, chalk becomes marble.*

Right: *Fossils of Ammonites found in sedimentary rock formations.*

There are many kinds of sedimentary rocks. Some are coarse mixtures called conglomerates. Others are finer grained sandstones, while still others, like chalk, are made from deposits of a single material. Limestone is made almost entirely from the remains of sea creatures.

The third type of rock is called **metamorphic**. This means that the original sedimentary rock has been changed completely by heat and pressure. Layers of sedimentary rock sink under their own weight towards the hot mantle. Some may get hot enough to melt at 600-700°C (1100-1300°F). Add to this the pressure of mountain building movement and the result is that chalk becomes marble and clay becomes slate. This process helps valuable minerals, present in the original rocks, to flow into veins, from which they can be mined.

The age of the earth

The knowledge of rock formations has enabled geologists to chart the last

ERA	PERIOD	AGE (millions)	EVENTS	LIFE	
CENOZOIC	QUATERNARY	2			
CENOZOIC	TERTIARY	3-65	HIMALAYAS AND ALPS FOLDED	FIRST MEN / DINOSAURS EXTINCT	1
MESOZOIC	CRETA-CEOUS	66-135	PANGAEA BREAKS UP	MAMMALS APPEAR	2
MESOZOIC	JURASSIC	136-190		AGE OF DINOSAURS / FIRST BIRDS	3 4 5
MESOZOIC	TRIASSIC	191-225		FIRST DINOSAURS	6
PALEOZOIC	PERMIAN	226-280	FORMATION OF PANGAEA	FIRST REPTILES	7
PALEOZOIC	CARBON-IFEROUS	281-345	COAL DEPOSITS LAID DOWN IN SWAMPY FORESTS	PLANTS AND ANIMALS ESTABLISHED ON LAND	8 9
PALEOZOIC	DEVONIAN	346-395			10
PALEOZOIC	SILURIAN	396-430	SOUTH POLE IN SAHARA		11
PALEOZOIC	ORDO-VICIAN	431-500	SEA COVERS MUCH OF EARTH'S SURFACE	FIRST FISH / INVERTEBRATE ANIMALS	12
PALEOZOIC	CAMBRIAN	501-570		FIRST FOSSILS WITH SKELETONS	13
PRE-CAMBRIAN		571-4600	FIRST CRUST OF THE EARTH FORMED		
PRE-CAMBRIAN		4600	EARTH FORMED		

Key to illustrations
1. Neanderthal man
2. Triceratops 3. Cycads
4. Archaeopterix
5. Stegasaurus
6. Ichthysaurus 7. Dimetrodon
8. Lepidodendron
9. Xenacanthus
10. Osteoplepis
11. Macrocystella 12. Sinuites
13. Tribolites

600 million years of world history. Sedimentary rocks hold **fossils,** impressions or casts of creatures that lived when the layer was being deposited.

Fossil evidence shows the succession of events, for example the emergence of the first water life in the Cambrian period, or the extinction of the dinosaurs at the end of the Mesozoic era. But accuracy has only become possible with the introduction of dating by means of **radioactive decay** (or **radio carbon dating**).

Rocks contain minerals which are radioactive. This radioactivity decreases at a constant rate. So, if the original level of radioactivity of an element like uranium is known, the length of time for which it has been decaying can be worked out.

This technique has made it possible to chart the history of the world back through the formation of the continents about 3,800 million years ago, to the birth of the world and the solar system about 4,600 million years ago.

Things to do

1. WHAT HAVE YOU LEARNT?

Junior
a) *The Ring of Fire is:*
   – a type of electric fire ☐
   – the belt of mountains and volcanoes surrounding the Pacific Ocean ☐
   – the oldest mountains whose volcanoes are now extinct ☐

b) *Plate Tectonics is:*
   – the study of the movement of the rigid plates which form the surface crust of the earth ☐
   – the latest development in dentures ☐
   – the magma on which the plates float ☐

c) *Igneous rocks are:*
   – the commonest rocks on the earth's surface ☐
   – the least common rocks on the earth's surface ☐
   – rocks that are changed by heat and pressure ☐

Intermediate
a) *Mountain building is:*
   – a continuous process ☐
   – a process that was completed long ago ☐
   – dependent on events like volcanic eruptions to keep it going ☐

b) *Continental Drift explains:*
   – how fossils move from one continent to another ☐
   – how the world was formerly covered with more land than water ☐
   – how the continents have moved and are still moving slowly on plates ☐

c) *The age of the earth can be estimated by:*
   – boring deep into the interior of the earth ☐
   – applying measurements of radioactive decay ☐
   – consulting ancient documents ☐

Advanced
a) *There is a clearly defined relationship between:*
   – the occurrence of volcanoes and the Ring of Fire ☐
   – the Mid-Atlantic Ridge and the Ring of Fire ☐
   – shield mountains and the Ring of Fire ☐

b) *Mountain building is a constant process involving:*
   – the emergence and decay of the edges of the plates ☐
   – the head-on collision of rigid plates ☐
   – the circular motion of the plates ☐

c) *Geologists are unable to make accurate projections about the earth's history further back than 600 million years because:*
   – fossil evidence is absent ☐
   – radio carbon dating cannot cope with such an interval ☐
   – there is no rock evidence available for study ☐

2. A HEAD FOR HEIGHTS

Junior
Sometimes it is difficult to calculate how tall one thing is in relation to another. By estimating, measuring or asking, find out:
a) how tall you are
b) how tall your house is
c) how high your school is
d) how high the nearest block of flats is

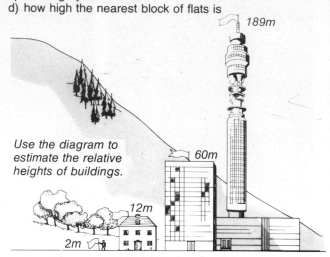

Use the diagram to estimate the relative heights of buildings.

Intermediate
In your local library look up the Ordnance Survey map covering your area. Find out:
a) The average height of the town where you live
b) Is the town on flat land, or are there variations in the height of it?
c) At about what height is the ground that your house stands on?
d) How far do you have to travel to reach high ground over 200m (656ft); over 300m (984ft); over 1,000m (3,281ft).
e) How high is the highest peak in Britain?

3. THE SHAPE OF THE LAND
Just as we find it difficult to judge relative heights, it is difficult for map surveyors to give us an idea of the height and shape of the land. One way of doing this is by representing height on maps by means of contour lines.

Junior
Look at the landscape in the sketch below. Contour lines have been superimposed so that it looks like a map.
a) Where are the contour lines closest together?
b) Where are they furthest apart?
c) What type of landscape is shown by contour lines:
   – very close together? very far apart?

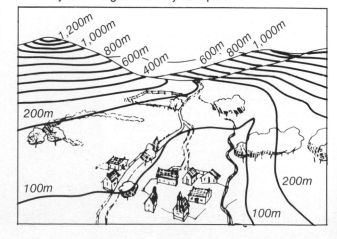

Intermediate

If you draw a cross section across contour lines as in the diagram below, it shows you the shape of the land.
a) What shape do these contours make?
b) Where are the houses located? Where is the main road?
c) Work out the gradient of the chairlift.

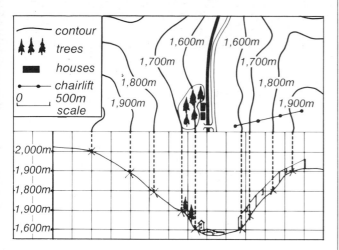

Advanced

Now look at the map on the back cover of the book.
a) By studying the photograph on the front cover carefully, try to locate on the map on the back cover exactly where the photographer was standing.
b) Give three ways in which the map makers have tried to give us an impression of the landscape of this area?
c) Can you think of any other ways of showing differences of terrain on a map?

4. THE MAKING OF BRITAIN'S MOUNTAINS

Three main mountain building periods occurred in Britain. The areas which they affected are shown in the map.

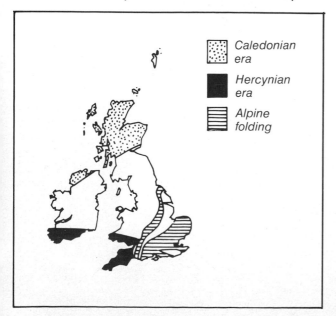

Junior

Match each of the periods to the parts of Britain in which they occurred?
a) Hercynian period   The Weald
b) Caledonian period   South Wales/South west England
c) Alpine period   Northern Scotland

Intermediate

Look up and explain the main features of each of the periods.

Advanced

Why was Britain strongly affected by the first two mountain building epochs and only on the fringe of the Alpine mountain building period?

5. UP IN THE MOUNTAINS

By looking at maps before you go or by getting information at your resort, try to find out the following:
a) The height of the airport at which you arrive.
b) The height of your resort.
c) The height of the highest peak in the region around your resort.
d) How does this compare to the highest peak in Britain?

6. PROJECT – A BALANCING ACT

The crust of the earth is just like an iceberg. We only see the tip which projects above the surface. To see how this occurs, cut blocks of the same wood into different shapes and heights. Float them in a transparent water container, perhaps a fish tank.

Wood blocks floating on water

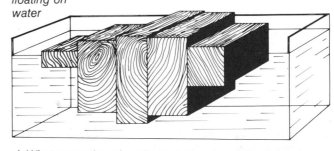

a) What proportion of each block appears above the surface of the water, and what proportion of it below?
b) Why do the blocks float in this way?
c) What are the similarities between the earth's crust and the blocks of wood floating in the water?

The blocks of wood are not attached to the surface of the water, but are kept up by the part which is beneath the surface. The earth's crust acts in the same way. Mountains are not attached to the surface of the earth, but have roots which project into the magma to a depth that is in proportion to the height showing above the surface. While the different parts of the earth's surface are all constantly moving, they remain more or less in balance. This process is called **isostasy**.

II. The Ice Age

Many of the interesting features of the mountain environment, such as the shapes of valleys, the outline of mountain peaks and the existence of certain lakes, are a result of ice ages which have occurred repeatedly over millions of years.

During the last Ice Age, which ended 10,000 years ago, there was three times as much ice covering the land as there is today. Although both Europe and North America were once covered by ice caps, today only the polar regions are under ice sheets. Europe's ice sheet was the size of Antarctica, spreading right over Scandinavia, across Germany and the North Sea and over most of the British Isles. The ice over Britain reached a thickness of 1,800m (6,000ft).

Europe in the Ice Age

The areas covered by the ice sheet were completely uninhabitable. South of the ice margin was a region where the ground was permanently frozen. This is known as the **permafrost zone,** and extended as far as the south of France. This region was bare tundra, an almost treeless plain of snowy grassland. In sheltered spots, a few birch or pine trees might have grown, but the growing season lasted only three months. Mammoths, woolly rhinoceri, bears and musk oxen roamed in the permafrost regions and provided food for the Neanderthal people who lived at this time.

The world since the Ice Age

By comparison with the Ice Age we live in comparatively mild times, known as an inter-glacial age. Nevertheless, over 10 per cent of the earth's surface is still covered by glaciers and ice caps. Today the great majority of the ice is in Antarctica, Greenland and the Arctic, covering in all about 15 million square kilometres (5.8m sq miles).

The world's longest glacier is the Lambert glacier in Antarctica. It is over 500km (300 miles) long. Most of the rest of the ice is found in glaciers in the world's mountain ranges. In the Himalayas and Karakorams, in Asia, some of the glaciers are 70km (45 miles) long. The longest glacier in the European Alps, the Aletsch (shown on the cover), is relatively small – at only 24km (15 miles) long.

Antarctica is the only part of the world which can show us today what the Ice Age ice sheet was like. Many nations have continuous research programmes in Antarctica and these

Swamp vegetation caused by poor drainage in permafrost areas.

Above: *18,000 years ago in the last Ice Age much of Europe and most of Britain was under ice.*

have revealed some amazing facts. Ice covers 95 per cent of the continent. Some of the ice is 3,000m (10,000 ft) thick, with lakes under it. Geothermal activity melts the lower layers, while the surface temperature can fall to −45°C (−49°F) and below.

It has been possible to map the high mountains beneath the ice by radio echo sounding. It was discovered that radio waves penetrated ice, when pilots were confused by inaccurate altitude readings. Their altimeters were giving them their height above the mountains, submerged under thousands of feet of ice. The surface of the ice sheet bears no relation to the shape of the mountains beneath it.

Antarctica was glaciated about 50 million years ago, when the continent of Gondwanaland split in two. The other half is Australia – as can be seen from the similarities of the coastlines of the Great Australian Bight and the Indian Ocean section of Antarctica.

Below: *In the permafrost zone, south of the ice, lived Musk Oxen, Mammoths, Reindeer, Polar Foxes and Woolly Rhinoceri. In sheltered spots there were a few birch and pine trees. Neanderthal people lived by hunting.*

Hills rounded by being covered by an ice sheet in a previous ice age.

A lobe of stagnant ice.

Dwarf birch trees mark the northern tree line.

The glacial landscape

Glaciers are nature's sculptors. During the Ice Age they gouged great troughs in mountain ranges like the Alps. The rocks and debris they removed from one place they deposited in another. The results are the jagged peaks, the deep valleys and many lakes which make alpine regions so attractive.

In other parts of the world, like Greenland, Alaska and Antarctica, there are still many glaciers, filing away at the landscape beneath them. In Europe only a few remain.

How glaciers begin

On high mountains snow falls. Snowflakes lying on the ground melt in the daytime sun and refreeze at night. Gradually they change into granules of crystallized snow called **névé** or **firn**.

More layers of snow fall. The extra weight of each layer compresses the snow underneath into ice. In the Alps this process may take 20 years. In the extreme cold of Antarctica it may take over 3,000 years.

The same thing happened at the beginning of the Ice Age, three million years ago. Snow fell on the hills and steep valleys of highland areas. As the snow piled up, the lower layers turned to ice. Finally the whole mass began to slide down the hills and into the valleys. The glaciers – often known as rivers of ice – were born.

Today's glaciers, like the Aletsch Glacier on the cover of this book, are small remnants of their Ice Age ancestors. The Aletsch is still the largest in the Alps. The evidence of their work can be seen in valleys from which they have retreated as the climate became warmer.

How glaciers work

As a glacier moves it causes erosion. This happens in two ways. The enormous weight of ice, carrying with it great lumps of rock and debris, sandpapers away the valley floor. This is called **glacial abrasion**.

When ice is subjected to pressure, it melts. Glacial ice can be pressurised by its own weight, or because it is being forced over or round an obstacle, like a rock outcrop. When the ice melts it drops the boulders it has picked up.

A glacier in a valley is like ice cubes in an ice tray. In both cases the cold ice freezes to the sides of its container – the tray or the valley. But the mass of the glacier is constantly moving, so that the ice plucks and tears away the rock to which it has frozen. This is called **glacial quarrying**.

Glacial abrasion makes a valley deeper and straighter by wearing away at the twists and turns of existing river valleys. Eventually the ice cuts off the lower ends of ridges that jut into the main valley. These are called **truncated spurs**.

Glacial quarrying produces many spectacular landscape features. A **cirque** is the name given to the upper end of a valley that has been gouged by the ice into a steep-walled circular shape, like a Roman amphitheatre.

When two cirques meet back to back the result is an **arête** – a jagged knife-edge of rock that falls away on either side into a cirque.

When three or more cirques meet back to back the result is a **horn**. The Matterhorn in Switzerland is the most famous example of this formation.

Above: *Where the Swiss Gorner and Grenz glaciers meet rock debris appears as streaks of moraine in the ice.*
Right: *A horn like the Matterhorn is formed when three cirques meet back to back. An arête (foreground) forms when two cirques work backwards towards each other.*

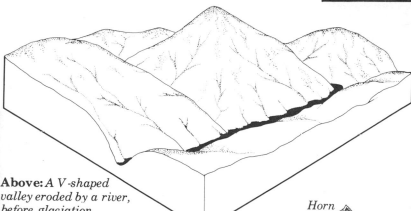

Above: *A V-shaped valley eroded by a river, before glaciation.*

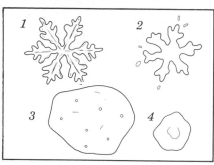

Above: *The process by which snow flakes are compressed into granules of névé or firn, which eventually forms into glacier ice.*

Horn

Cirque

Arête

Arête

Truncated spur

Glacier

Medial moraine

Hanging valley

Ground moraine

Left: *The Mer de Glace glacier in the French Alps, over 14km (8.5 miles) long. Note:* **A** *Lateral moraine;* **B** *Medial moraine;* **C** *Truncated spur;* **D** *Scree;* **E** *Cirque;* **F** *Arête;* **G** *Crevasses.*

Above: *The same valley during glaciation. The V-shaped valley has been turned into a U-shaped valley. The lower ends of ridges that jut into the main valley have been cut off to form truncated spurs.*

When glaciers retreat

In places, which were under glaciers long ago, it is possible to see what a great effect ice had on the landscape. There have been at least five major periods of glaciation, or ice ages, during the last two million years. The last ice age ended only ten thousand years ago. Today we live in inter-glacial times. During the periods of glaciation, up to thirty per cent of the earth's surface was covered in ice. Today only ten per cent of the world is under ice. As ice is one of the most powerful forces working on the earth, there are many after effects of glaciation still to be seen today.

Glacial erosion

Glaciers have two ways of changing the surface of the earth. They may erode the land under the ice or they deposit the debris elsewhere. Some of the results of glacial erosion are shown on the previous pages. It is possible to see arêtes, horns and truncated spurs while a glacier still occupies the bottom of a valley. But some of the after-effects of glaciation can only be observed when the ice has melted completely.

Roches moutonnées are rounded off lumps of bedrock, over which the glacier has passed. The side of the rock facing the flow is rounded and often covered in deep scratches. These are caused by the ice dragging other rocks over the obstacle in its path. The down-glacier side of the roche moutonnée is steep, jagged and broken. The ice would have plucked pieces off it in passing.

In some places it is possible to see glacial grooves, channels cut into solid rock, up to 100m (325ft) wide. Although **cirques** can be seen where glaciers begin, before they retreat, the true shape of a cirque can only be seen when the ice has gone. Scotland and the Lake District have some excellent examples.

The **glacial trough**, or U-shaped valley, is also an obvious result of glaciation. The V-shaped valley caused by river erosion is gouged out by the ice, leaving a wide valley bottom and steep cliffs at the sides. Small valleys running into the main valley are frequently cut off high up, leaving **hanging valleys,** with waterfalls plunging over the cliffs down to the main valley floor.

Glacial deposition

The vast quantities of debris moved by glaciers have to be deposited somewhere. Ice can transport rocks over great distances. Rocks from Norway have been found in England. These rocks are called **erratics.** Some 15 per cent of the earth's surface is covered with debris from previous ice ages. The **glacial drift,** as the debris is known, can be 400m (1,300ft) deep.

The glacier has two ways of depositing its load of rock. Where ice melts at the end, or along the side of the glacier, rocks of all sizes and shapes that were bedded into the ice are dropped. This material, which contains everything from fine sand to rocks the size of several houses, is known as **till.**

The now outdated term, boulder clay, is no longer used. Till can be laid down by the glacier as a fairly even layer, called **ground moraine,** or in piles. These ridges often form at the end of a glacier, where the ice melts and releases its load of debris. If a glacier then retreats, the **terminal moraine** can form a dam for the meltwater. Lake Garda in northern Italy is at one end of a U-shaped valley dammed by a terminal moraine. Deposition can also take place under the ice. **Drumlins** are oval-shaped mounds, which are formed from debris deposited under a glacier.

Meltwater streams are the other agent of glacial deposition. The bottom of a glacier often has water under it. This water runs down hill as a stream, taking debris with it. An **esker** is a ribbon of gravel, following the bed of stream that once flowed under the ice. In Finland there are eskers many miles long and 30m (100ft) high. Where there was a lake under the ice, mounds of gravel called **kames** were deposited.

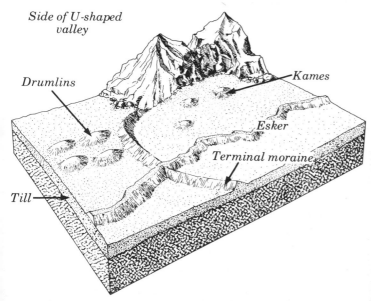

Side of U-shaped valley

Drumlins

Kames

Esker

Terminal moraine

Till

Top right: *Haweswater Tarn, Cumbria, is an example of a glacially gouged cirque.*

Above: *Cross section of the end of a glaciated valley, showing typical deposits.*

Left: *Eskers are gravel ridges deposited by glacial meltwater streams. Finland has eskers hundreds of kilometres long.*

Right: *How ice smooths one side and plucks out the other side of a roche moutonnée.*

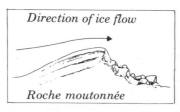

Direction of ice flow

Roche moutonnée

Right: *A stream cuts into till laid down by a glacier. Above are the cliffs of the Bellegarde Valley, France. Nearby glacial deposits are quarried for roadstone.*

Wearing away the mountains

As well as glaciers, other forces, like water, wind, heat and cold, all gradually destroy rock, in a process known as **weathering.**

Because of their height, mountains tend to receive more extreme weather conditions than lowlands. A great deal of rain and snow falls on them. Strong winds blow round them. The temperature in the mountains can be quite high, or very low. As a result, exposed rocks are broken down comparatively quickly.

Two forms of weathering

Weathering breaks down rock in two ways. **Physical weathering** is largely caused by **temperature changes** and **frost.** When rock, that has been cooled overnight, is heated by the sun, it expands. As it expands it is likely to crack along weak joints. Eventually the cracks become so large that pieces of rock fall away.

When water becomes ice the volume of the water increases by nine per cent. So, when rain or melted snow drips into a rock fissure and then freezes at night, the ice often splits the rock apart, just as it can burst a water pipe in winter. In high mountains this shattering of rock can produce a **rock sea,** or Felsenmeer in German. The ground is littered with angular blocks of stone.

Chemical weathering is a more subtle process. Water contains certain minerals. When rain falls on certain types of rock, the minerals in the water can react with minerals in the rock. An example of this is the way in which iron rusts when in contact with water. In mountains the water dissolves some minerals in rocks and washes them away.

Agents of erosion

Once the process of weathering has loosened small pieces of rock, the agents of erosion, **wind, water, ice** and **gravity,** carry them away. Water, wind and ice also wear away the surface of the earth as they move. Pages 18 and 19 show how ice leaves its mark on the landscape. Similarly, wind can produce some spectacular effects, exploiting weak points in the rock to hollow out caves and even make natural bridges.

In dry places, the wind carries sand along with it at great speed, causing desert sand storms. The sharp particles of sand carried on the wind beat against the rock and wear it away. This is known as **sand blasting.** The same process is used industrially and for cleaning buildings.

Water begins its work of erosion as rain falling on rock. On steep slopes it washes out the smallest and softest particles of rock, leaving only the larger and harder ones. **Earth pillars,** tall columns of rock, protected at the top by a harder boulder, are a result of this process.

Gravity does not actively erode mountains, but when a particle of rock is detached from the hillside, gravity will make sure that it falls away, sometimes hundreds of metres, to the valley floor. Below high cliffs, from which frost detaches blocks of stone, piles of loose rock accumulate. This is called **scree.** In some places the rocks fall into the valley, forming a cone shape, called a **talus.**

Landslips

Almost any steep slope can be subject to landslip. So, in mountain areas **landslips,** or **landslides,** are very common. Every year landslips cause damage to crops, buildings, roads and railways.

Landslides can be divided into three broad categories. **Rockfalls** occur when solid rock is detached from a steep hill or cliff. This often happens where the strata are not level but tilted, making a slide for the top layer of rock. Even on the gentlest of slopes, the surface layer is always on the move. Evidence of this **soil creep** can be seen in the way in which earth accumulates on the uphill sides of hedges and walls. On steeper slopes, after heavy rain or during a rapid thaw, **earthflows** can occur. These are slow movements of soft material on a vast scale, or the result of rockfalls, in which case they can be waves of semi-liquid debris moving at terrifying speed.

A combination of a rockfall and its resulting earthflow caused one of the world's worst landslide disasters of recent times. In 1970 a mass of ice and rock at the summit of the highest peak in Peru, Huascaran, collapsed. The flow of debris apparently travelled at over 300kph (160mph), in a wave over 75m (250ft) high, down the Rio Shacsha Valley. On its way the wall of moving mud destroyed two small towns and one large town, Yungay.

The Huascaran disaster was caused initially by an earthquake. Rain and frost can also cause landslips. But man's activities are also one of the principal causes. Cutting trees, the roots of which held together the surface soil, can cause slips. So, too, can

engineering works, like tunnels and quarries. In 1966, the coal mine slag heap at Aberfan in Wales collapsed killing 116 children in school.

River erosion

Rivers help carry away the rock fragments produced by weathering and they also have erosion patterns of their own. In general rivers erode the landscape into **V-shaped valleys,** as opposed to the U-shapes produced by glaciers. But the steepness of the V and the shape of the valley bottom can be altered by many factors. If the river follows the path of a glacier, it may make little change in the U-shape left by the ice. On the other hand, if it is cutting through soft material, it produces a steep V-shape. Where the river spreads out into a flood plain, the characteristic flat valley floor is not caused by erosion, but by deposition of the load of sediment it carries.

The higher the mountains, the greater the effects of **denudation** (the combined effects of weathering and erosion). Research suggests that the Himalayas are being denuded at a rate of about 1m (3ft 3ins) every 1,000 years. In the Alps the rate is nearer 0.5m (1ft 9ins) per 1,000 years, while in lowland areas it can be as little as 1cm ($\frac{1}{2}$in) in 1,000 years.

Left: *Scree, small particles of rock broken away by frost action.* **Top right:** *This river of mud and rock, almost 10 miles long and 1,000m wide, devastated a whole valley in Peru in 1970.* **Above:** *A V-shaped valley caused by river erosion.* **Bottom right:** *Earth pillars protected from erosion by caps of hard rock.*

Things to do

1. WHAT HAVE YOU LEARNT?

Junior

a) *An ice cap is:*
 – a hat for protection against the cold ☐
 – the frozen peak of a mountain ☐
 – the shrunken remnants of former ice sheets ☐

b) *The thickness of ice over Britain reached:*
 – 600m (2,000 ft) ☐
 –1,800m (6,000 ft) ☐
 –1,200m (4,000 ft) ☐

c) *The main animals in the permafrost zone were:*
 – woolly rhinoceri ☐
 – polar bears ☐
 – reindeer ☐

Intermediate

a) *The characteristics of the ice sheets can be reconstructed by:*
 – altimeters ☐
 – geothermal activity ☐
 – radio echo sounding ☐

b) *Neanderthal Man lived by:*
 – cultivating the land during the short summer season ☐
 – hunting animals with primitive weapons ☐
 – fishing like present-day Eskimos ☐

c) *Glaciers are formed by:*
 – an accumulation of snow turning lower layers into ice ☐
 – rain freezing on impact with very cold land surface ☐
 – cirques working backwards to meet each other ☐

Advanced

a) *The surface of the ice sheet bears:*
 – a close relationship to the relief beneath it ☐
 – no relationship to the relief beneath ☐
 – the exact shape of the land covered by ice ☐

b) *A glacier erodes by:*
 – abrasion and meltwater ☐
 – inflation and flowing water ☐
 – deflation and pressure jets ☐

c) *Evidence of the distance that ice moved is provided by:*
 – erratics ☐
 – remnants ☐
 – roches moutonnées ☐

2. LIVING IN THE ICE AGE

About 10,000 years ago (a mere blink of the eye in geological terms) most of Britain was covered by ice. Only parts of southern England were not covered by the ice sheet. Even here it was bitterly cold and the vegetation was tundra, similar to that found in Siberia or northern Canada today. These conditions are known as **periglacial**. Only the top few inches of the ground thaw out in the short summer season.

Underneath the earth is still frozen solid, so it is known as **permafrost** (permanent frost).

Junior

Imagine what it was like living in a cave in southern England when the ice had reached its maximum limit, without even the most basic comforts of modern living. What would you have had to eat? Where would your clothes have come from? How would you have kept warm?

Intermediate

Find out as much as you can about the way of life of the Eskimos, Lapps and other peoples who live in periglacial environments today?

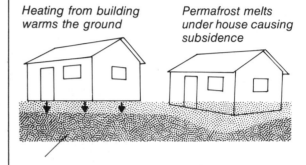

Heating from building warms the ground

Permafrost melts under house causing subsidence

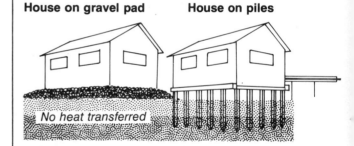

House on gravel pad

House on piles

No heat transferred

Advanced

The diagrams above show how modern technology has enabled people living in periglacial settlements to adapt to these extreme conditions.

a) What effects does the thawing of the top layer of the ground have upon buildings?

b) How do the people combat the problems caused by permafrost? Think of the services that are laid beneath our houses and streets. It is virtually impossible to dig in permafrost, as the ground is like concrete, so what happens to the water supply, sewerage and other pipes?

3. BRITAIN UNDER ICE

Glaciers and ice sheets transformed dramatically the land which they covered. Most of the cutting and carving of the typical shapes, such as U-shaped and hanging valleys (page 17), occurred as the ice advanced. Most of the deposition of material, forming drumlins and moraines, for example, occurred as the ice retreated (page 19).

5. ANATOMY OF A GLACIER

This diagram (called a **glacier budget**) brings together a number of facts about glaciers already mentioned on pages 16–19. Study it and try to answer the following questions.
a) What causes a glacier to move?
b) How does a massive thing like a glacier move?
c) What happens if the source of snow is reduced or disappears?
d) What does a glacier carry?
e) How does it obtain what it carries?
f) How can a glacier carry this material?
g) Why does it eventually lose this material?
h) In what way could a glacier be likened to a human being?

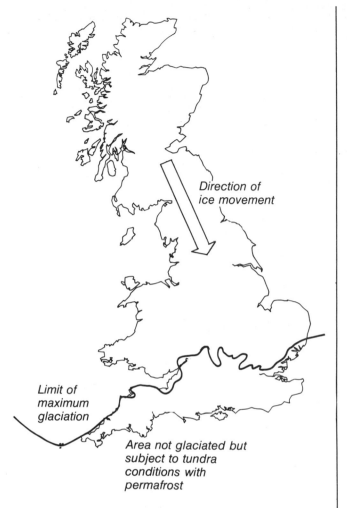

Direction of ice movement

Limit of maximum glaciation

Area not glaciated but subject to tundra conditions with permafrost

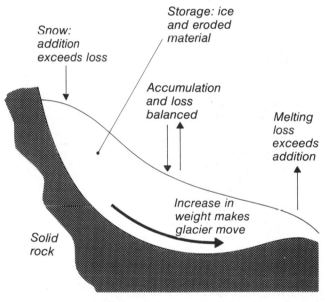

Snow: addition exceeds loss

Storage: ice and eroded material

Accumulation and loss balanced

Melting loss exceeds addition

Solid rock

Increase in weight makes glacier move

Junior
Look at the map above. Was the area where your house or town is submerged by ice during the last great Ice Age?

Intermediate
Is there any evidence of the work of ice in, or near, your home? Are these features caused by glacial erosion or deposition?

Advanced
On the journey to your resort and during your stay make a note of all the glacial features you can recognise.

4. NATURAL DISASTERS

Here is a list of famous disasters. Say what caused each of them. If you can, describe the event in your workbook.
– Pompeii 79 AD
– San Francisco 1906
– Krakatoa 1883
– Tokyo 1923
– Aberfan 1966
– Central Italy 1980

6. PROJECT – MAKING A GLACIER

It is possible to make a model to simulate the behaviour of a glacier.

In a three-sided box, mould a valley out of plaster of Paris. Make it as realistic as possible, by starting with a narrow, steep-sided section and gradually widening it out further downstream.

When this has set, prepare a bucketful of a mixture made from two parts kaolin (China clay) and one part water. Pour the mixture slowly into the upper part of the valley, so that it begins to flow downstream under its own weight. Keep feeding it at regular intervals until the mixture reaches the end of the valley.

As it flows the pattern of crevasses and faults should quickly become clear.

Place powdered coke or cork on the edge of the mixture along the valley sides and it will be carried downstream and moraines become evident. Matchsticks can be placed on the surface to calculate the speed of movement.

If the glacier does not flow, either the mixture is too thick, or the plaster of Paris is not slippery enough. Thin the mixture and/or grease the surface of the valley and tilt the model to about 20° from the horizontal.

III. All about snow

Winter in the mountains invariably brings snow. When the temperature falls to freezing point (0°C, 32°F) the water vapour in the clouds becomes ice crystals. These vary from 0.07mm to 0.2mm in diameter. They are mainly hexagonal in shape, particularly at low altitudes where water vapour is plentiful. At higher altitudes, where water vapour is scarce, the crystals are often rod or cone-shaped. These crystals do not fall to earth individually. They cluster together in bunches about 2.5mm across to form **snowflakes.**

The snowline

Above a certain height on a mountain, snow covers the ground all the year. This level is known as the **snowline.** Below this line accumulated snow melts. Above it the snow remains, even in summer.

The position of the snowline varies considerably from place to place. In general, the altitude of the snowline is lower the further the mountain is away from the Equator. Thus, the snow line on Mount Kilimanjaro, in East Africa, which is only 3° from the Equator, is about 5,600m (18,400ft); whereas in Norway, which is 68°N, the snowline is at about 1,065m (3,500ft) The average snowline in the Alps is at about 2,750m (9,000ft), but this varies from summer to winter. By the end of September snow covers the mountain down to 2,130m (7,000 ft) and by November, to 610m (2,000ft).

In spring, the snow melts more rapidly on sunny, south facing slopes. In summer it is not uncommon to find

At freezing point (0° C, 32°F) water vapour in clouds becomes snow crystals. Each one is 0.2mm in diameter, or less. The crystals bunch together to form snowflakes, which are about 2.5mm across.

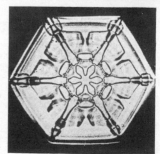

nothing more than an occasional patch of snow on a sunny ridge at a height of 3,650m (12,000 ft) whereas the slope, on the other side of the valley, is deep in snow from a height of 2,450m (8,000 ft).

A boon and a hazard

Freshly fallen snow is almost 90 per cent air. It forms an effective, insulating layer, reducing heat loss from the ground below and keeping the temperature of the soil quite constant. This is particularly important to farmers.

When the snow on the fields finally melts, the ground is often free from frost and ready for planting. Similarly, when the snow on the pastures melts, the water is absorbed into the soil and encourages the growth of fresh, new grass.

Snow is not always such boon. Indeed, it is more often disruptive. Many Alpine valleys have snowfalls of over 7.5m (25 ft) and in parts of the Rockies, in North America, 12m (40 ft) is not uncommon. Moreover, wind may blow the snow into drifts of twice

this depth. Many road passes in the Alps are blocked by snow for over half the year – from November to mid-May or June. Trains and planes are often delayed by heavy snowfalls.

The sheer weight of snow can also be dangerous – so much so, that in countries such as Canada and Switzerland, there are strict building regulations which stipulate that roofs must be built to support a certain weight of snow per square foot. In the Alps, the total weight of snow a roof may have to bear may be as much as 30 tonnes.

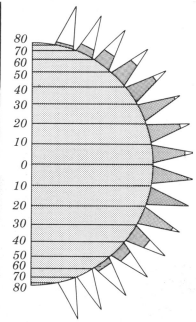

80
70
60
50
40
30
20
10
0
10
20
30
40
50
60
70
80

The snowline is the point above which the snow remains all the year. Its altitude depends on the distance from the Equator. It also varies between the Northern and Southern hemispheres. On Mount Kilimanjaro, 3° from the Equator, the snowline is at 5,600m (18,400ft). In Norway at 68°N it is 1,065m (3,500ft). The diagram on the left shows the relative height of the snowline at various latitudes north and south of the Equator.

Left: *Snow on roofs can cause damage because it is extremely heavy.*
Above: *Galleries protect some roads, like the Simplon Pass, but even here snow has to be cleared at times.*
Right: *Snow insulates the ground, making it easy for farmers to plough in spring.*

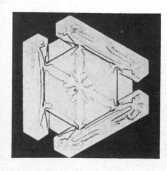

Avalanches

Avalanches are one of the hazards of high mountains. They consist of a mass of sliding snow or ice which moves with great force. There are several things which determine when, where and whether an avalanche is likely to happen.

Firstly, it depends on the depth of freshly-fallen snow. If there is sudden, heavy snowfall, the risk of an avalanche is greater, because the new snow does not hold on to the old snow straight away. Snow falls of 100cm (40ins) or more are particularly dangerous.

In 1951, for example, 125cm (50ins) of snow fell in 24 hours in the Bedretto valley, in the Alps, and started 26 big avalanches in three days. Luckily, no-one was killed.

Generally, avalanches only start on steep slopes (with a gradient of more than 22°) although, once set in motion, they may travel right across the gentler slopes of the valley floor.

In winter, particularly in the Alps, avalanches usually happen on the shadier – the northern and eastern – slopes of a mountain. Here the snow takes longer to stabilise, because the temperature is lower. By contrast, in spring, the sunshine melts the snow on the south facing slopes first, often causing avalanches.

Dry snow avalanches

There are two main types of avalanche – dry-snow and wet-snow. **Dry-snow avalanches** are the most dreaded. These generally happen in winter, with terrible suddenness, when the winds are at their strongest. Wind, swirling round a peak, will blow a heaped mass of fresh snow into the air. If and when the wind drops suddenly, the snow falls in a great cloud down the slope. The snow displaces enormous amounts of air, **pressure waves**, which may travel at speeds of over 300km (187 miles) per hour. These blasts of air are often more destructive than the avalanche itself. They can be sufficiently strong to uproot trees and demolish buildings outside the area swept by the avalanche.

Slab avalanches are also unpredictable. These may be started by sudden movements, such as a fall of stones or by a person passing by. The frozen top crust of snow breaks off in a slab, often 20m (65ft) or more wide. As it slides, it splits up into a mass of snow blocks.

Wet snow avalanches

The most common type of avalanche is known as the **wet-snow** or **ground avalanche**. These happen when the temperature starts to rise in late winter and early spring. They are formed of the compact snow, called névé or firn, which has lain on the ground all winter. As the snow melts, it loosens its hold on the ground underneath. This heavy, mushy, wet snow

slides down the mountain slopes at great speed, often tearing up rocks, grass and soil in its path. Thousands of these avalanches happen regularly each year – in some places the avalanches have even been given names! They usually follow specific tracks, known as **chutes**, and the mass of snow, ice and debris ends piled up high on the flatter slopes.

Prevention and protection

In regions which are prone to avalanches, many ways have been devised to prevent them. In Switzerland there is a Federal Avalanche Research Institute, constantly working on the problem. On some steep slopes, where deep snow is known to accumulate, metal fences are built. This is, however, expensive. More commonly, controlled explosions are set off to trigger small, harmless avalanches which might otherwise have become larger, destructive ones. In the Rogers Pass, in the Rockies, the Canadian Army maintains permanent gun-emplacements, used for shooting down potential avalanches.

In high risk areas, new buildings are now constructed to withstand the force of an avalanche and there are often warning systems which tell people to evacuate their homes in good time before the onset of an avalanche.

Top: *People buried under avalanches must be found as soon as possible, because they may run out of air. Searchers sound the avalanche with long thin poles to see if there are any people underneath.* **Above:** *Dogs can scent people buried under several feer of snow and are usually the first to find survivors.*

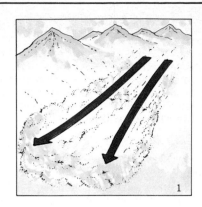

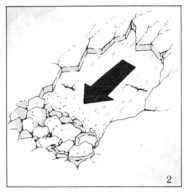

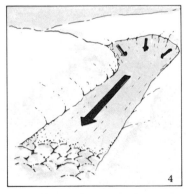

Above: *Swiss steel and concrete avalanche prevention fences.*
Left: *An avalanche in the Swiss Alps. For an idea of the size of the avalanche, look for the ski-lift pylon in the middle of it.*

Above: 1) *Dry snow avalanches create dangerous blasts of air.* **2)** *Slab avalanches occur when a snow crust breaks off.* **3)** *An unconfined ground or wet snow avalanche.* **4)** *A wet snow avalanche channelled in a valley.*

Mountain climate

No two parts of any mountain valley have exactly the same climate. According to the altitude of a particular spot and its aspect (which direction it faces), it may be wetter, colder or windier than a place only a mile away.

Effects of altitude

As you climb higher, the temperature drops, the air becomes thinner, the winds become stronger and yet you are more likely to become sunburnt. Why should this be so? The temperature drops at a rate of about 1°F for every 300 feet or 1°C for every 150 metres you climb. At the same time the sunshine becomes more intense. One of the reasons for this is the thinness of the air at high altitudes. For example on the top of a mountain 2,500m (8,200ft) high there is less than half the dust, half the moisture and only three quarters of the oxygen and carbon dioxide in the air than at sea level. This means that the sun's rays can pass through the atmosphere much more easily.

You might expect therefore that the sun's rays would be much more powerful and make the air at the top of the mountain that much warmer. The sun is indeed stronger because fewer of its **ultra violet rays** are filtered out. Ultra violet rays are the ones that give you sunburn. That's why skiers and people who live in the mountains have such tanned faces.

But in spite of this the air temperature is lower, because it is not really the rays of the sun that warm the air. Air is mainly warmed by heat reflected from the ground – it is warmed from below. During the day rock surfaces are grilled by the sun, even though the air is cold. The rocks and the ground radiate the heat back to warm the air. At night the rocks cool again very quickly.

Winds and rain

Mountain slopes are often windy. For example, winds at a height of about 600m (2,000ft) travel three times as fast as winds at ground level, sometimes reaching speeds of 160kph (100mph). During the day, winds generally blow up the slopes (because warm air rises). These are called **anabatic winds**. At night, when the air cools and becomes heavier and denser, the winds blow down the slopes. These are known as **katabatic winds**. They are funnelled down into the valley and this is where they are at their strongest.

In general, mountains have higher rainfall than lowlands. Warm air can hold more water vapour than cold air.

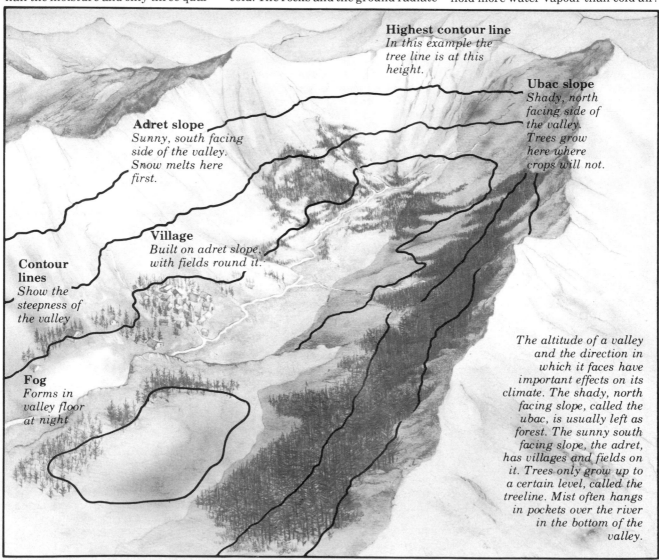

Highest contour line
In this example the tree line is at this height.

Ubac slope
Shady, north facing side of the valley. Trees grow here where crops will not.

Adret slope
Sunny, south facing side of the valley. Snow melts here first.

Village
Built on adret slope, with fields round it.

Contour lines
Show the steepness of the valley

Fog
Forms in valley floor at night

The altitude of a valley and the direction in which it faces have important effects on its climate. The shady, north facing slope, called the ubac, is usually left as forest. The sunny south facing slope, the adret, has villages and fields on it. Trees only grow up to a certain level, called the treeline. Mist often hangs in pockets over the river in the bottom of the valley.

As warm air is forced upwards, it expands and so cools. Water vapour in the air condenses and falls as rain. At very high altitudes, and especially in winter, it falls as snow instead.

In valleys which point in a north-south direction, both sides receive equal amounts of sunshine. In valleys which run from east to west, the situation is quite different. The north facing slope will lie in heavy shadow, while the south facing slope is bathed in light and warmth. In the southern hemisphere, though, north-facing valleys are sunny.

So distinct are these differences, that they have been given names. (French: **adret and ubac**, Italian: **adretto and opaco**, German: **sonnenseite and Schattenseite**).

Because of these differences in warmth and light, the slopes are used quite differently. The shady ubac slopes are often left in their natural state as pine and spruce forest whereas the sunny adret is cleared for crops, hay meadows or grazing. Villages and chalets are more often situated on the adret.

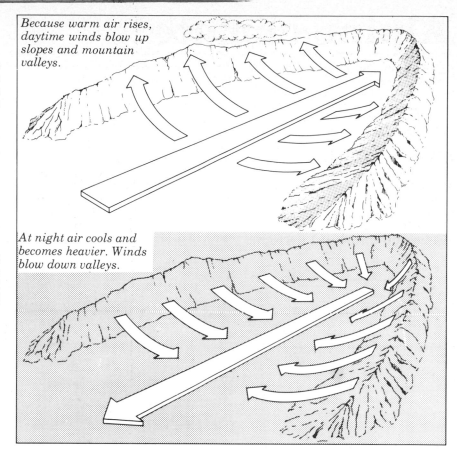

Because warm air rises, daytime winds blow up slopes and mountain valleys.

At night air cools and becomes heavier. Winds blow down valleys.

Temperature inversion

In mountain areas you may notice that there is often fog or mist at night. This is due to a process known as **temperature inversion.**

Generally, during the day, the higher up you go, the colder it is. But at night the reverse is often true. During the day the sun warms the earth in the valley, which in turn warms the air by radiation. When the sun has gone down the last of the warm air rises from the ground into the atmosphere and the ground becomes cold. As the air cools above the valley, water droplets form and turn into fog or mist. The mist forms a blanket separating the cooler air on the valley floor from the last of the warm air higher up the mountain.

The diagram opposite shows how this cycle can be repeated every 24 hours.

Temperature inversion can occur in any valley, but the effects are more exaggerated in mountain regions, with high peaks and deep valleys, which trap the fog.

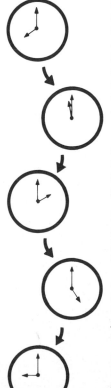

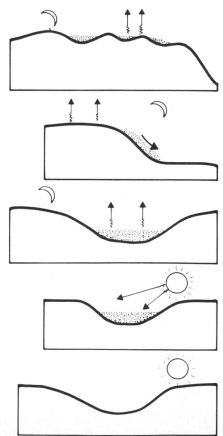

8.00pm: *At the end of the day exposed areas of land warmed by the sun radiate heat up into the atmosphere. As the air cools, water droplets form, causing fog in the hollows.*

Midnight: *The fog has spread, creeping down into the valleys, where the ground has cooled.*

2.00am: *Fog shrouds the valley floor. Above it the air is still warm.*

5.00am: *The rising sun heats the top surface of the fog, gradually dispersing it.*

9.00am: *By mid-morning the sun's warmth has cleared the fog completely.*

Alpine climate

Like all mountain areas the Alps influence their own weather, because of their height. They also act as a barrier between the weather systems of northern Europe and the Mediterranean, preventing cold air from reaching the Po valley, in Italy, and preventing warm air from the south reaching southern Germany.

However, the Alps are not an impenetrable barrier to the weather. Sometimes a layer of air passes over the peaks. As air is pushed upwards, the moisture it contains turns to rain. Once over the mountain summit, therefore, the air is dry. And as it loses altitude, going down the other side, it warms up. This dry, warm, down-slope wind is called the **föhn**.

When air comes overland from the north, it is not very moist. So it produces light rain on the northern slopes of the Alps, before descending the southern slopes as the **north föhn**. This happens mostly in winter.

Much more noticeable in its effect is the **south föhn**. A mass of warm, moist air rises up over the Alps from the Mediterranean. This produces heavy rain on the Italian side of the mountains. But by the time it reaches the northern slope it is blowing very strongly (up to 130kph, 80 mph) and it is dry and warm. As a result it can raise temperatures very smartly – by up to 12°C (22°F) in a few hours.

The south föhn blows chiefly in the spring and autumn, bringing clear, warm weather to the northern slopes of the Alps. In spring this helps to thaw the last of the snow and in the autumn it helps to ripen the last crops. However, it does bring problems. Sometimes the thaw can be too fast, causing floods.

Because of the föhn, and the barrier effects of the mountains, the northern, Swiss and Austrian, side of the Alps has quite a different climate to the southern, Italian, side. In the south it rains harder and more, as a result of the föhn, but on fewer days of the year, than in the north. The south receives most rain in spring and autumn. The north has rain in the summer.

The central, east-west valleys of the Alps have a climate of their own. They receive much less rain than either the north or south slopes.

Right: *the föhn blows warm air from the Mediterranean over the Alps.*

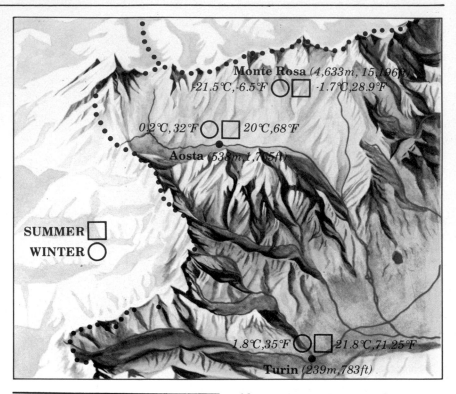

Monte Rosa *(4,633m, 15,196ft)*
-21.5°C, -6.5°F ○ □ -1.7°C, 28.9°F

0.2°C, 32°F ○ □ 20°C, 68°F
Aosta *(538m, 1,765ft)*

SUMMER □
WINTER ○

1.8°C, 35°F ○ □ 21.8°C, 71.25°F
Turin *(239m, 783ft)*

Comparing north and south

	Rain (1 yr.av.)	Rain (days)	Sun (hours)	Cloud (av.cover)
N	1,200mm	140	1,485	65%
S	1,800mm	105	2,286	50%

Above: *Air warms or cools according to altitude, changing by about 1° for every 150m height difference. This is called the lapse rate. The figures show the temperature, summer and winter, at various altitudes.*

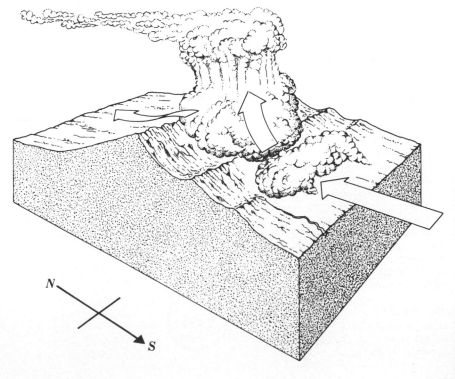

N

S

Things to do

1. WHAT HAVE YOU LEARNT?

Junior
a) *The snow line is:*
   - a special express for skiers ☐
   - a line marked in the snow to identify a ski run ☐
   - the height above which snow covers the ground permanently ☐

b) *Snow assists the farmers by:*
   - protecting the ground from the glare of the sun ☐
   - keeping the ground free from frost ☐
   - melting at the same time each year ☐

Intermediate
a) *The temperature at which water vapour turns to ice crystals is:*
   - 0°C (32°F) ☐
   - 32°C (0°F) ☐
   - 1°C (34°F) ☐

b) *As you climb a mountain, the temperature decreases because:*
   - the air becomes thinner ☐
   - fewer of the ultraviolet rays are filtered out ☐
   - there is less oxygen and carbon dioxide in the air ☐

Advanced
a) *The height of the snowline is generally:*
   - higher in the northern than in the southern hemisphere ☐
   - higher in the southern than in the northern hemisphere ☐
   - at the same height in both southern and northern hemispheres ☐

b) *Avalanches are more likely when:*
   - there is fresh snow on shadier slopes ☐
   - there is old snow on sunnier slopes ☐
   - the temperature suddenly increases ☐

2. WEATHER REPORT

If you listen to the weather forecasts on the radio or television, you will hear the following expressions. What has happened to make these warnings necessary?
- "Drivers are warned to take particular care, because black ice is making driving conditions hazardous."
- "A combination of heavy snowfalls and high winds causing drifting has blocked all roads over the Pennines."
- "Dense fog has closed Heathrow and Gatwick airports. Aircraft have been diverted to Stansted and Luton."

Junior
Imagine that you are preparing weather warnings for transmission over the radio or television, but this time for the mountainous area around your resort. Write down at least four warnings you could broadcast, taking into account the special weather conditions in the area.

Intermediate
Look at the diagram showing the annual **precipitation** (rain and snow) in part of the Valais area of Switzerland.
a) Where is the highest rainfall?
b) Where is the lowest rainfall?
c) Why does the rainfall differ between these two places?
d) What effect will these differences have on the use to which the land is put and the way of life of the inhabitants?
e) Where would you expect most people to live? Why?
f) Where would you build a storage reservoir for hydro-electricity? Why?

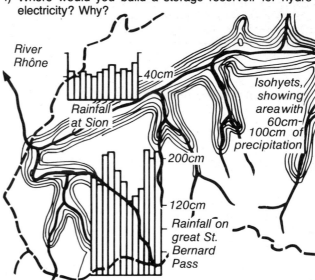

Advanced
Look at the diagram below and answer the following questions.
a) What happens to the temperature as the height increases?
b) Using the answer to the previous question, describe what effect height has on temperature?
c) What happens to rainfall as height increases?
d) Describe what happens to the 0°C isotherm in the Swiss Valais at different times of the year.
e) Why is the 0°C isotherm found at lower levels in the summer than in the winter?

The line on the graph shows the height at which a 0°C (32°F) temperature occurs in the Valais throughout the year.

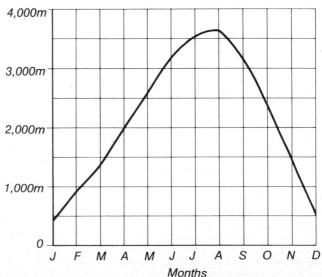

Mountain safety

Mountains can be dangerous places. In Europe, few people live above 1,500m (5,000ft). The altitude and the cold make the mountain environment hostile to man. Yet, increasingly, recreation takes people into the mountains. In the winter they ski in vast numbers. Estimates put the number of British skiers at about 800,000 and the number of French who ski at between two and three million. In the summer, Alpine resorts, which were once deserted between April and December, are now thronged with walkers, climbers and campers.

Winter and summer

Ski resorts take every care to ensure that the skiing is as safe as possible. **Pistes** or ski runs are marked clearly for skiers to follow.

Skiers themselves must make sure their clothes provide good protection from wet and cold. Clothes trap a layer of still, warm air next to the body. If

Above: *An RAF Wessex rescue helicopter in action in Wales.* **Left:** *A rock climber scales a sheer rock face.* **Far right:** *In France the Gendarmerie Nationale maintain mountain rescue experts at 22 centres.*
Right: *Stretcher bearers of the Gendarmerie Nationale on mountain rescue exercises near Chamonix.*

bare skin is exposed, especially in a wind, the **chill factor** takes effect: a wind of 40 kph (25mph) at –7°C (20°F) is the equivalent of calm air at –22°C (–8°F). One of the easiest ways to lose body heat is to ski bare-headed.

It is also important to be fit. If skiers have done the correct exercises beforehand, they will have enough stamina.

You also need **ski sense** – a close relative of common sense with a little specialist knowledge. The winter safety code will help here.

Summer visits to mountain regions also have their potential dangers. Walkers need to be equipped with good, warm clothing, proper **boots**, **maps** and a **cautious instinct**. It is very easy to be lost, or slip, or be out longer than anticipated. Climbers, of course, have their own special needs and rules.

Mountain rescue

The first mountain rescue organisations go back to the days of the Roman Empire. Caligula established a village

on the Little St Bernard Pass, in order to help travellers. The Benedictine Hospice on the Great St Bernard Pass, with its famous dogs, has helped travellers for hundreds of years.

Today mountain rescue teams are made up of both volunteers and military personnel – The Royal Air Force Search and Rescue Organisation in Britain, and the Gendarmerie Nationale in France, for example. They are equipped with radio, helicopters and tracker dogs. They play a key role in mountain safety, as more and

Winter safety code

*Never ski alone – Always ski in groups of at least three – one to stay in case of accident, one to go for help.

*Watch out for other skiers – don't ski near ski classes, people may not be able to get out of the way; overtake wide and uphill of other skiers; give priority to slower skiers and those downhill of you; if you stop or fall, look behind and then move out of the way.

*Observe official signs – if a run or lift is closed, there is a good reason.

*Always ski within your own ability – dare-devil skiers can injure others as well as themselves.

*Don't walk on the piste – your footprints can be dangerous to others.

*If you do not have ski stoppers, make sure your ski safety straps are fastened – runaway skis can kill.

*In fog or a whiteout – do not go out; if you are skiing already, head for the nearest safe point, like a lift station; don't walk straight down the hill, there might be a cliff.

*Don't stop in narrow places or where other skiers may not see you.

*If there is an accident – send for help (lift stations have phones), indicating exactly where you are; show position of injured person by sticking crossed skis into the snow; keep person warm, but don't move him.

Summer safety code

*Check your equipment – boots, clothes, maps, ropes, ice-axes etc if needed.

*Plan your route – so you know how long you will take, leaving a good safety margin.

*Make sure you are fit enough (and skilled enough) to make the walk or climb you propose.

*Find out about the weather forecast.

*Never go alone, even on short rambles – it is very easy to lose the way.

*Take an emergency pack – some food, a torch, a compass; make sure you know the distress signals.

*Respect the environment – don't leave litter, damage plants, pollute water, risk a fire.

> The international mountain distress signal is six long calls, whistles, or flashes with a light, in succession, at one minute intervals. The reply is three calls with a one minute interval.

more people visit mountain areas.

In 1979 the National Alpine Rescue Corps of Italy was called out 161 times in Piedmont alone. They helped 174 people, saving 144 of them. Most of their work was in summer. In winter each resort tends to deal with most of its own emergencies. Twenty one per cent of the people the Italian Rescue Corps helped had slipped from a track or path (good boots count); 15 per cent had lost their way (maps are essential); 11.5 per cent were taken ill (fitness counts); 7.5 per cent slipped on

snow and ice; 7 per cent were caught by bad weather and another 7 per cent were victims of ski accidents.

Apart from injury, there are two main causes of illness in mountains – altitude and cold. **Hypothermia** (loss of body heat by exposure to extreme cold) lowers an individual's morale and resistance and can eventually kill. The best prevention is good mountain clothing. **Altitude sickness** is caused by a lack of oxygen in the atmosphere at great heights. In Europe few people reach the heights at

which the lack of oxygen is dangerous. And if they do, they don't stay long. But in places like Peru mountain people have adapted to living at over 3,500m (12,000ft), developing extra large hearts and lungs. Some people are more susceptible to the effects of altitude than others. Whether you are affected or not also depends on how quickly you go up. On the Lima-Oroya railway in Peru, which climbs from sea level to 4,783m (15,683ft) attendants spray sufferers with pure oxygen from a cylinder.

IV. Mountain flora

It is remarkable that any flowers at all can survive on the high mountain peaks. Much of the year they are attacked by fierce and freezing winds, heavy frost and are covered in deep snow. Yet as soon as the snow melts, small plants are found colonising the rocks, making rock gardens that are quite the equal of the prize winning, man-made rock gardens at horticultural shows. High mountain flowers have a special attraction all of their own, possibly because the plants found growing in such inhospitable surroundings seem so fragile and delicate.

Adapting to altitude

In fact Alpine plants are often very resilient, being well adapted to the specialised conditions of their environment. These conditions vary according to **vegetation zones** at different altitudes.

At the tops of the mountains, plants are often very small, because the high concentration of ultra violet light at high altitude produces short stemmed plants with small leaves, although they have large and brightly coloured flowers. In shady areas in the woods there are plants like lilies of the valley, which like shade. In the hay meadows lower down there are displays of brilliantly coloured orchids and other flowers.

The cold, the snow and the short summer are all problems that plants in mountains have had to adapt to. Alpine flowers can grow even before the snow melts. Heat produced through the chemical processes of plant cell growth melts the snow around the growing tips of the plant. The young shoots grow very rapidly. In spring, near the snowline, the first crocuses and soldanellas (Alpine bells) can be seen growing in melt holes, surrounded by snow.

In the highest places, the summer growing season for plants can be as short as two months in the northern Alps and four months in the southern Alps. **Annual plants**, which depend on setting and ripening seed for the continuation of their species, have adapted by speeding up the process of seed production.

The glacier buttercup holds various records. In Norway it has been known to produce its white flowers only five days after the snow has melted from the plant and to have ripe seeds only 17 days later. The glacier buttercup is also the highest known flowering plant in Europe. It has been found at the summit of the Finsteraarhorn in Switzerland at 4,275m (14,025ft). It only grows at very high altitude – above 2,000m (6,500ft) in the Alps. The only places in which it can be seen lower down are near glacier tongues.

In fact many high level plants can be found where glacier ice comes down between the peaks.

Flowers and computers

Near Obergurgl in Austria there is a high altitude research hut, where, using computers, there has been continuous recording of details about individual glacier buttercup plants for over 20 years. Their respiration and photosynthesis are measured. As a result it has been discovered that the plants can stay alive, although buried under snow continuously for several years.

Suddenly, in a good summer, the snow round the plant melts. Within a few days it is in flower. And even more amazing, it is likely to be covered in many more flowers than normal, as if to make up for lost time.

Most Alpine plants are **perennials**, which means that they come up year after year. They develop long roots, penetrating deep into rock crevices, anchoring them against being blown or washed away. Even trees have adapted themselves to live in these extreme conditions. High in the Alps there are dwarf willows, with tiny leaves and stems, growing horizontally, pressed to the surface of the rock. They are very slow growing – a tree only a few inches high could be half a century old.

Below left: *Highest growing plant in Europe, the glacier buttercup.*
Above: *Sulphur anemone growing near Zinal. Common up to 1,500m.*
Below: *The spring gentian only opens when the sun is shining.*
Right: *Moss campion with a gentian in the centre of the cushion.*
Far right: *Alpine soldanella. The heat from the growing tip of the plant melts the snow around it.*
Below right: *Dwarf willow tree.*

Vegetation zones

Every part of the earth has a natural selection of plants and animals, specially adapted to suit its environment. One of the best ways to see how the selection of living things changes with the change of environment is to look at the vegetation zones of a mountain.

As you climb from bottom to top, you can see the gradual changes taking place. On the lower slopes of the Alps there are warm climate trees and crops, like lemons and maize. Further up there are trees and crops that prefer cooler, damper conditions, like beeches and barley, while at the top of the mountain only hardiest rock plants can survive.

Many different things contribute to the selection of flora and fauna that live in any one spot. The winter and summer temperatures, the winds, the altitudes, the type of soil, the aspect, the latitude, among others.

The vegetation zones in the Alps vary from north to south, because the northern slope of the mountains has a colder climate than the southern slope, which is influenced by Mediterranean weather systems. The föhn, too, has an effect on the Alpine zones, bringing warming winds to the north and heavy rain in the south.

The diagram below shows various vegetation zones typical of the Alps. But there are many local variations. In general, the higher the area, the shorter the growing season, and the more resilient the plants and animals must be to survive. The lower slopes have the warmth and water to support deciduous trees. Further up the hardier coniferous trees take over. Their waxy needle leaves lose less water and are less easily damaged by frost. Higher up still, snow can insulate plants against the wind and frost of winter. But the extra ultra-violet light and the lack of soil mean that only low plants with sparse foliage survive.

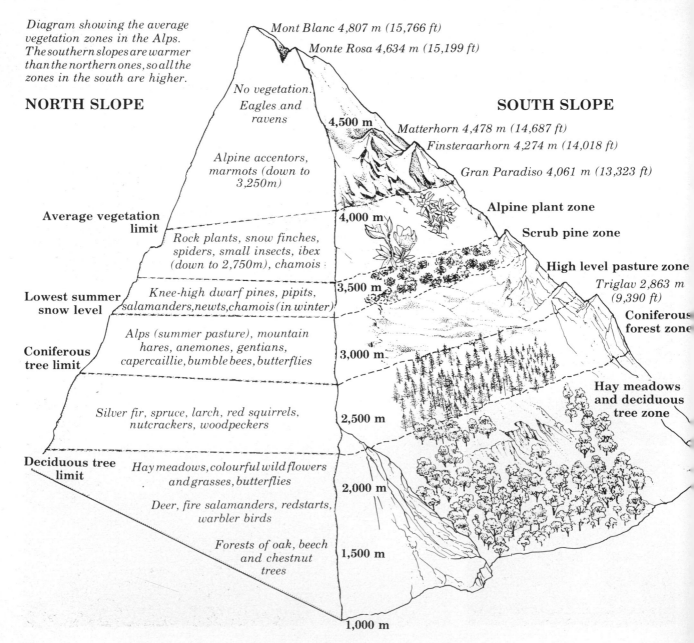

Diagram showing the average vegetation zones in the Alps. The southern slopes are warmer than the northern ones, so all the zones in the south are higher.

NORTH SLOPE

SOUTH SLOPE

Mont Blanc 4,807 m (15,766 ft)
Monte Rosa 4,634 m (15,199 ft)

No vegetation. Eagles and ravens

4,500 m

Matterhorn 4,478 m (14,687 ft)
Finsteraarhorn 4,274 m (14,018 ft)
Gran Paradiso 4,061 m (13,323 ft)

Alpine accentors, marmots (down to 3,250m)

Average vegetation limit

4,000 m

Alpine plant zone

Scrub pine zone

Rock plants, snow finches, spiders, small insects, ibex (down to 2,750m), chamois

High level pasture zone

Triglav 2,863 m (9,390 ft)

3,500 m

Lowest summer snow level

Knee-high dwarf pines, pipits, salamanders, newts, chamois (in winter)

Coniferous forest zone

Alps (summer pasture), mountain hares, anemones, gentians, capercaillie, bumble bees, butterflies

3,000 m

Coniferous tree limit

Silver fir, spruce, larch, red squirrels, nutcrackers, woodpeckers

2,500 m

Hay meadows and deciduous tree zone

Deciduous tree limit

Hay meadows, colourful wild flowers and grasses, butterflies

2,000 m

Deer, fire salamanders, redstarts, warbler birds

Forests of oak, beech and chestnut trees

1,500 m

1,000 m

Ecology and conservation

Most of men's activities in the mountains have an effect on the environment – and not many of them improve it. However, in the past, before mountain areas were developed for industry and tourism, life there was extremely hard. If men wish to benefit from modern development they must live with the mountain environment.

The importance of conservation in the mountains was first recognised at the beginning of this century. In Switzerland in 1909, the Nature Protection League instigated the creation of the National park, near Zernez, just over the border from the Italian resort of Livigno. Since then this area of 16,000 hectares (40,000 acres) has been carefully protected.

The enormous Gran Paradiso National Park in Italy (58,000 hectares, 143,000 acres) was opened in 1922. Today it has 65 full time rangers to look after it day and night.

Although these, and other national and regional parks, do provide natural havens for flora and fauna, in other places they are under constant attack.

The ecological system of the mountains is very fragile and it can be upset easily. The first plants to grow below the permanent snowline are mosses and lichens. They are tiny, non-flowering plants, which find nourishment from damp rock surfaces. As they grow, spread and die their leaves and stalks crumble and collect as dust in pockets of rock. New plants grow in this damp dust. Wind-blown particles catch in the plants. Gradually soil builds up, allowing flowering plants' seeds to germinate and establish themselves.

It is a very slow process. Some plants' roots eventually crack the rocks, which are further crumbled by frost action, so adding nutrients to the soil. The name of the saxifrage family of plants, common in the Alps, means stone-breaking in Latin. They are part of a natural cycle thousands of years long.

Modern man is destroying this cycle. Smoking factory chimneys pour sulphur dioxide into the atmosphere, where it dissolves. The result is that in parts of Europe it actually rains dilute sulphuric acid. In the past 200 years rainwater has changed from neutral, to an acidity which can be measured as ph 2.4.

This acidity kills plants. Lichens in particular are very sensitive to atmospheric pollution. Insects too are affected by air pollution. Ladybirds, normally red with black spots, are found instead to be black with red spots in places where the air is heavy with industrial smoke.

Smoke that might be blown away in flat country, is trapped by deep mountain valleys, concentrating the effects of the pollution. At Saint Jean de Maurienne, in Savoy, France, the huge aluminium smelter puts out fluorine, which becomes fixed in plants and animals' bones. The vegetation has been affected too and killed off in some places. This process is quickly followed by small landslides. Eventually, if this is allowed to happen on a large scale, it can cause collapse of the whole structure of the environment.

In Canada in 1976 there were 10,358 forest fires, destroying 2.1 million hectares of trees. In 1980 there were twice as many fires.

An aluminium smelter near St. Jean de Maurienne in France.

Be a good ecologist

Do not:

Drop litter — litter that seems to disappear quickly into the snow is one of the greatest environmental hazards caused by skiers. When the snow melts in spring, the line of each ski lift is marked by a trail of rubbish.

Metal rings from drinks cans can cause great danger and pain to animals that eat them.

Plastic bags are dangerous as well as ugly.

Glass bottles can cause fires, or even trap small animals that enter them.

Pick flowers — leave them for other people to enjoy seeing them as you saw them — growing.

Disturb or frighten animals — if you chance upon a fawn hidden in the undergrowth keep away. Its mother will not be far off. If you touch it, leaving a human scent on its coat, its mother may abandon it.

Do anything to cause a fire — Some mountain areas become very dry in summer and forest fires can start extremely easily. Once started, they not only damage valuable forest, they kill many small animals.

Do:

Learn about what plants and animals can be seen. Look for tracks and signs in the snow or on the ground.
Find out about local conservation laws. Many areas have strict local regulations to protect the environment, especially National Parks and Nature Reserves.

> **Take nothing but pictures.**
> **Leave nothing but footprints.**
> **Kill nothing but time.**

Mountain fauna

Animals have been forced to **adapt** in order to survive harsh mountain conditions. Living in the lowlands is often easier and more comfortable, but it is also more crowded – not only with other animals. The human population has expanded and uses more and more space. The two principal characteristics that mountain animals have developed are **agility** and a **warm coat,** but sometimes even these are not enough. Since 1960 the European brown bear has been almost extinct. Only a few still exist in the Pyrenees, Scandinavia and Eastern Europe. For centuries the bears were hunted and trapped, so that now only a few remain in mountain national parks.

National parks have helped another mountain animal – one of the most agile of all. At the end of the last century the ibex was virtually extinct. But in 1922 Victor Emmanuel II, King of Italy, created the Gran Paradiso National Park, where the ibex lives successfully today.

The ibex has long, heavy, backward-curving horns. The ridges on them are growth rings, showing the age of the animal. The hooves of the ibex give it extraordinary agility. The hoof is steel-hard, but the underside is covered with rough hairs, enabling the ibex to walk forwards, or even backwards, up near vertical slopes. A startled ibex makes a noise like a short sharp sneeze.

Chamois, too, have hooves specially adapted for balance on slippery and steep slopes. They can sometimes be seen feeding on grassy patches among high rocks, but they are very alert to danger, signalling each other with nothing more than a single stamp of the foot.

Winter hibernation

Hibernation enables many mountain animals to pass the winter in the comfort of a burrow – up to 15 of them together in the case of the marmot. Marmots are large rodents (about the size of a cairn terrier dog), with a thick coat of hair. In summer they live on the sunny, boulder-strewn pastures above the treeline, occasionally sitting up on their hind legs to look around, while feeding on roots and grass. The classical writer Pliny called marmots mountain mice, but when they whistle they can be mistaken for humans, making a shrill, piercing noise. Marmots often live to 20 years old.

Many mountain animals manage to survive the winter without hibernating. Some, like the chamois, move to lower, more sheltered places during the winter months. Others grow a thicker coat, or even a **white coat,** to **camouflage** them in the snow.

Although the squirrels in the Alps appear almost black, they are in fact the red squirrels that were once com-

mon in Britain as well. In some valleys squirrels have rust red summer coats, with white fronts. In winter they live in trees on lower slopes and sometimes go scavenging through resort litter bins.

The mountain hare changes its colour in a more spectacular way. In November long white hairs begin to grow over its grey-brown summer coat. This provides a double thickness for warmth and such a good disguise that it is very difficult to see the hares against the snow.

Mountain birds

Golden eagles are still to be seen soaring overhead in the Alps. They need a very large territory to provide for themselves and their young. Where the borders of Italy, Austria and Switzerland join, pairs of eagles frequently nest in a different country each year; The characteristic deep croak of the raven is often heard in mountain areas, or the call of the Alpine chough, which is also black, but with a yellow bill.

Other exciting birds to watch out for are snow buntings, redstarts, woodpeckers, crested tits in the conifer woods in winter, and the largest of all the game birds, the blackcock, which is used as the symbol of the Aletsch Glacier Nature Reserve, shown on the cover of this book.

Other creatures have found all sorts of ways of coping with mountain conditions. The Apollo butterfly is a strong flyer able to battle with high level winds. It also has a furry body which holds whatever heat the sun provides. Alpine salamanders are shiny black reptiles about 7-10cm (3-4ins) long. They need a moist skin to breathe, so in fine weather they only move at night. But on rainy days they can be seen walking with their slow stiff-legged gait. They live in the wet woods, or river gorges above the trees up to 3,000m (10,000ft). Even the temporary ponds left by melting snow in spring are occupied – by newts and croaking frogs and toads.

Right: *Pairs of golden eagles live in many parts of the Alps. They need a very large hunting territory, covering several valleys.*
Below right: *The Apollo butterfly is a very strong flyer, enabling it to live high in the Alps. This one was found at over 4,000m in Kashmir.*
Below: *The marmot lives in a burrow all the year round, hibernating in it in the winter, up to 15 at a time. Marmots live on plants and roots.*
Below left: *A family group of ibex. At the beginning of this century the ibex had been hunted to near extinction. Now they are protected, living at great heights in national parks.*

Things to do

1. WHAT HAVE YOU LEARNT?

Junior

a) *A vegetation zone is:*
   – a place to grow vegetables ☐
   – an area where certain plants and animals
     adapted to the environment ☐
   – the way the mountain is divided ☐

b) *Animals in mountainous areas have two special charac-*
   teristics, they are:
   – agile with warm coats ☐
   – camouflaged and fast ☐
   – easily seen and stealthy ☐

c) *Many mountain animals hibernate in winter which means*
   that:
   – they go to sleep ☐
   – they eat more to keep warm ☐
   – they move to a warmer climate ☐

d) *Most alpine plants are:*
   – annuals ☐
   – dormant ☐
   – perennials ☐

Intermediate

a) *The highest known flowering plant is:*
   – edelweiss ☐
   – glacier buttercup ☐
   – Alpine bell ☐

b) *Mountain animals have adapted to the conditions in a*
   number of ways including:
   – developing thick skins to keep out the cold ☐
   – having a higher than usual body heat ☐
   – thick furry coats often with double layers ☐

c) *Conservation in mountains is aided by:*
   – an expensive advertising campaign ☐
   – the designation of National Parks ☐
   – isolating endangered species for special
     protective measures ☐

d) *Flora and fauna vary at different heights because:*
   – only certain species can survive the climatic
     conditions at particular heights ☐
   – certain animals and flowers prefer certain
     types of soil ☐
   – experts have landscaped the slopes to enhance the
     enhance the scenery ☐

Advanced

a) *Clothes keep people warm by:*
   – trapping a layer of still warm air next to the body ☐
   – adding extra weight ☐
   – keeping out cold winds ☐

b) *Mountain-top plants are small because:*
   – of a high concentration of ultraviolet light ☐
   – there is less nourishment in the thinner soil ☐
   – the rocks at this height are more crystalline ☐

c) *Coniferous trees are found at higher altitudes than*
   deciduous trees because:
   – they are shallower rooting ☐
   – their leaves lose less water and are
     less easily damaged by frost ☐
   – the waxy leaves allow snow to slide off easily ☐

d) *The increase in tourists has had adverse effects, such*
   as:
   – taming formerly wild animals ☐
   – increasing the numbers of rodents ☐
   – assisting the virtual extinction of certain species ☐

2. MAN IN THE MOUNTAINS

One of the biggest threats to the flora and fauna of the
mountains in recent years has been the tourist invasion. To
meet the demand for leisure facilities a large number of
purpose-built complexes have been built in previously
remote places. This diagram of a proposed development
shows some of the dramatic effects that this can have.

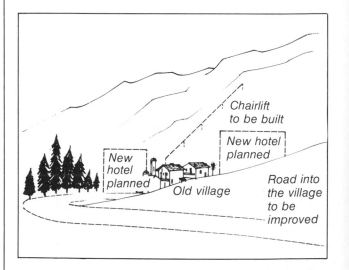

Junior

Copy the plan into your workbook. Add all the features you
can think of that would transform it from an isolated hamlet
into a modern tourist resort. Some of the additions have been
drawn in as outlines to start you off. Remember to make a
key for your plan.

Intermediate

Make a flow diagram to show what kind of jobs are created
with a new hotel complex. For example it is calculated that 20
guests generate work for one waiter. Look at the diagram on
page 48 for an idea of how the diagram should work.
a) Which of these new jobs requires skills which have to be
   imported from outside the village?
b) Which of these new jobs do not require special skills or
   training and will give employment to the existing population?

Advanced

Imagine you are meeting to discuss the proposed development. Below is a list of the people who might be involved in or affected by the project. Members of the class can each pick a character from the list or you may prefer to discuss one as a group and appoint a spokesman for your point of view.

Mr. Agostini's family has had a small farm in the village for generations. He owns a chalet and a small herd of cattle which produces sufficient milk, butter and cheese to support his family. He also has a few small hay fields around the village.

Mr. Bernard is the representative of the company interested in the site. He believes that the quaintness of the village and the magnificent scenery will attract tourists, so he wants to buy up as much land as he can for development.

Miss Carissa has just left school and cannot decide whether to stay in the village or go to the city to look for a job. The arrival of tourism might allow her to stay at home, find a good job and enjoy herself.

Mrs. Donna has run the village store for years. She keeps a small stock of most goods. They cost a little more than they do in the nearest large town, but her shop is convenient and saves time and petrol. A new resort could mean competition from modern smarter shops, but might also bring more customers for her.

Mr. Giovanni owns the local garage, but turns his hand to anything from coach hire to selling farm machinery. He already has plans for enlarging and modernising his premises and is busy thinking up even more schemes to make money from the tourists.

---

3. POLLUTION WATCHDOG

One of the greatest dangers to the mountain environment comes from pollution. You have read on page 37 how industrialisation has turned rain into dilute acid, but this is only one type of pollution. The illustration show many more sources of pollution.

a) Make a list of the different types of pollution shown in the illustration.
b) Which are caused by people and which by vehicles?
c) What steps do you think should be taken to prevent these different forms of pollution?

4. TREE SPOTTING

From a distance pine trees often look the same, but you can tell the difference between them by examining the way the needles grow. All the trees below are **coniferous** (they produce cones) and some of them are pines. Which ones could you see near your home and where? Which ones could you see in the mountains? Give yourself two points for everyone you can spot.

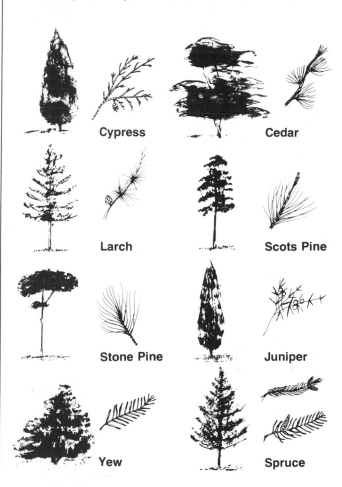

Cypress   Cedar

Larch   Scots Pine

Stone Pine   Juniper

Yew   Spruce

5. PROJECT – ECOLOGY

Copy the outline of the vegetation zones diagram on page 36 into your workbook and mark on it as many as possible of the following:
a) The highest point in the region around your resort.
b) The name and altitude of your resort in the appropriate place and whether it is situated on a north or south facing slope.
c) The boundary of:
the highest deciduous trees; the highest coniferous trees; the highest pasture; the highest hay field; the altitude of any mountain huts; any birds or animals you see; the height at which you find various flowers.
d) How does your diagram vary from the one on page 36? Try to explain the differences.

V. Mountain farmers of the world

Thousands of years ago, when primitive people were hunters and gatherers, before they learned to cultivate crops, they moved from place to place, following herds of wild animals. Later they tamed some of the animals they hunted. Cattle, sheep, goats and pigs all became domesticated. Both sheep and goats are originally mountain animals. The chamois, the mountain goat, is still hunted today.

In many areas of the world, especially mountains and deserts, there is not sufficient fertile land to support a settled community with its domesticated herds and flocks. People, therefore, move their animals from one pasture to another, so they can eat whatever grass is available.

These people cannot raise crops, because they move about. Therefore all their wealth is in their animals and the products made from them. They drink milk and make cheese from it. Some drink animals' blood as well. Their clothing is made from sheep's wool or goat hair (mohair), and some fabrics and wool they sell. Their tents are made from cow hide. Beef, lamb or goat meat is the mainstay of their diet.

Symbiosis

These people live in a state of **symbiosis** with their animals. Each is dependent on the other. The animals would die without the herdsmen to find them new pastures. The people would die without the animal products.

Many tribes still live like this today. Their lives are extremely hard. The Kirghiz, for instance, live on a plateau at between 4,000 and 5,000m (13,000 – 16,000 ft) in Afghanistan. Heavy snow covers the ground for over half the year. In winter the temperature falls to -40 °C (-40 °F). It is impossible for them to grow crops; they depend entirely on their animals – yaks, sheep, goats and Bactrian (two hump) camels.

The life of a nomad

Although people like the Kirghiz are **nomads**, wandering from one place to another looking for pasture, their travels are far from aimless. All nomadic peoples follow quite well defined routes, so that they are in more or less the same place at the same time each year. They know where there is likely to be good grass, and which places they must leave as a reserve for harsher times.

Sometimes this means making long journeys. The Bakhtiari are a nomadic group made up of several tribes in

Iran. Some of them migrate 250 miles between their summer and winter quarters. They pass the summer in the high pastures of the Zagros Mountains. Their journey from the coastal lowlands is long and hazardous. Animals often drown in rivers swollen with melting snow, freeze to death in sudden blizzards, or fall off narrow paths in high passes.

Other people all over the world make similar, but mostly easier journeys. Often they migrate between a dry zone, which has what little rain there is in winter, to a wet zone like the mountains, where there is water in summer. Following this pattern, Nepalese herders take their yaks up to over 5,000m (17,000 ft) in the Himalayas; Bedouin tribesmen of Morocco take their goats high into the Atlas mountains and Patagonians take their llamas and sheep up into the Andes, in South America.

Transhumance to survive

Moving livestock from one region to another according to the season, is called **transhumance**. And this is just what farmers in the Alps have done for generations.

Winter in the mountains is severe. The sun may reach a village in the valley bottom for only a few hours each day. Snow covers the ground from November-December to April-May. The animals are sheltered in barns, feeding on hay made the summer before.

As soon as the snow melts, the farmer mucks out the barns, spreading the manure on the hayfields nearby.

As soon as possible the cows are moved up the mountain, leaving the valley fields for growing crops and hay.

Immediately above the valley floor, there is often a steep hillside covered in trees. Above this there is likely to be a flatter area, beyond the treeline, where there is good grass in summer. This is called the **alp**, or **mayen**. A member of the farmer's family stays up there with the cows, as a daily journey to the village would be too long. The cows must be milked every day and cheese made from the milk.

Before winter comes again, the cows walk slowly down the mountain. If the hay crop has been good, there will be more than enough feed for them until next spring.

Transhumance like this is still practised in the Alps today. The farmers there follow a style of life that is closely related to the nomadism of the Bakhtiari or Kirghiz tribes.

Left: *Like many nomadic mountain people the Kirghiz tribe in the Karakoram Mountains live on the products of their animals. Their tents and clothes are made of hide and wool.*

Below: *They eat the milk, cheese and meat provided by their yaks.*

Above right: *They herd their yaks from low winter pasture to high summer grazing country.*

Below right: *The Bakhtiari people of Iran migrate up to 400km (250 miles) from the Zagros mountains to the coastal lowlands.*

The Alpine farmer

Many European mountain farmers still practise a form of transhumance, but not one that the Bakhtiari tribe would recognise. Modern transport and communications have made important changes, for the better and the worse.

The farmer's year

Winter: The weather in mountain areas has not changed, so the farmer must still keep his animals inside for about six months of every year.

He lives a more comfortable life than his grandparents lived, often with television, central heating and seasonal work as a ski instructor. His farm may be in a resort like Livigno, where there are cattle barns on the main street, near the hotels and the ski lifts.

Spring: Once the snow on the lower slopes has melted, the cows are turned out to graze. But not for long. These lower slopes are needed for making hay to feed the cows in winter. As soon as possible the cattle begin the journey up the mountain.

They used to make the trip on foot. The lead cow had a large bell which tolled a rhythm for the others to follow. Nowadays the animals are moved by truck. In Provence, in France, sheep are known to suffer from a respiratory disease, because they make the journey to the mountains in hours, whereas they used to have days to become used to the altitude.

Summer: Whole families used to move up the mountain to a summer village, called a borgo in Italy. And sometimes there were several settlements at different heights, right up to the snow line which the cows reached in mid-summer. The men and children (in the school holidays) still have the lonely job of looking after the cattle in the highest places. They live in little huts and spend their days milking and making cheese.

Autumn: During September and October the cows make the journey back down the mountain. The animals are strong and healthy, ready for winter and the next breeding season, or for further fattening on lowland farms, or for sale at the autumn markets.

Right: *In summer cows feed on the lush grass of the alp, above the tree line. Herdsmen milk them to make cheese and butter.*

Just as there are ceremonies and festivities for the departure in spring, so the return is celebrated in autumn. Markets are often an excuse for a fair.

By November animals and people are again under cover, ready for the onslaught of winter.

Transhumance in the 1980s

Today, comparatively few people make the journey to the alps or mayen, the high pastures. Transhumance is not everyone's ideal way of life. In Piedmont it is well known that many farmers are bachelors – women will not marry a man who is away for half the year. Often it is the old people who keep the farms going, while younger people work in town factories. In some cases one man takes charge of several farmers' animals for the summer, renting highland pasture from mountain villagers who no longer use it. Twenty years ago in northern Italy, a farmer might have had ten cows. Today there are fewer farmers but each has 50 to 100 cows.

The government encourages transhumance with a grant of 100,000 lire for each cow making the trip. The alpine grass is rich in nutrients, which are good for the cow and her milk yield.

Italy has particular problems in maintaining traditional mountain farming. If you fly over the Alps to land at Turin or Milan airports you will see how suddenly the mountains drop away to the plain of the River Po. Although the hills are steep the valley cities are very close to the mountain villages. People do not have far to go if they wish to earn good wages in a Fiat factory at Turin, or an Olivetti factory at Ivrea.

Recognising this the EEC is providing money to help develop mid-mountain farming. Instead of moving from the valley floor to the highest alps, farmers are encouraged to clear and farm land half way up the mountain. There they can grow hay in the summer and visit their cattle daily, without having to live in remote huts.

In Switzerland and other mountain regions, the problem of de-population is not so extreme, which is partly because the industrial areas are not so close to the mountains.

On the alp: *June-Oct, cows move up to snow-line and back. Milk made into cheese.*

On the lower slopes: *April-May, cows calving, grazing near village. June-Sept, hay making.*

Round the village: *Nov-Mar, animals in barn fed with hay; cows produce small amount of milk. April-May, ploughing and sowing arable crops. June-Aug, cultivating crops, vegetables, fruit. Sept-Oct, harvesting crops.*

Right: *A girl carries hay in a traditional conical basket, specially shaped to put most weight on the shoulders, like a modern rucksack. Similar baskets are used in the Himalayas.*

Above: *The cow giving the most milk is decorated with garlands and the biggest cowbell, before it is led down to the valley.* **Above right:** *Milking machines speed up the milking of cows.* **Right:** *Modern mini truck specially designed to be driven easily up steep slopes. The wheels are set wide apart for extra stability.*

Crops and farming methods

The traditional farming method of transhumance is almost entirely concerned with producing animals – with good reason. Land in mountain areas like the Alps is generally too steep, infertile and high for growing cereal crops. About one third of the Alps are barren rock slopes, lakes and glaciers. Another third is covered with forest. Of the last third, about 90 per cent can only be used for grazing. Other mountain regions suffer from the same problems. In Ladakh, India, only one acre in ten can be farmed.

A recent survey in the Rhone-Alps region of France revealed much about the difficulties of mountain farming. Each hectare (2.47 acres) of mountain land produces only 62 per cent of the value of the regional average. The majority of mountain farmers have to look for another job, or a business to help them make a living. Tourism often provides business opportunities.

Mountain farmers have various ways of overcoming their difficulties. In some cases they have altered the land. And in others they have specialised in crops that do well in mountain regions.

Terracing

In order to make steep land flat, and so easier to work, hill farmers all over the world have built terraces. Terraces are built like steps, levelled out with a retaining wall to stop the surface soil being washed away. Unfortunately terraces are almost always small, making mechanisation awkward.

The Incas of Peru were master terrace builders. In the Karakorum mountains of Asia, terraces go up to 3,000m (10,000ft). In the Philippines and Indonesia rice is grown in vast terrace systems.

In the Alps many villages have terraces nearby. In the summer crops are grown on them; and in winter, in places like Sauze d'Oulx, Bardonecchia and Chiesa-Caspoggio, skiers use them as nursery slopes. Above the approach roads to many resorts, vines can be seen growing on terraces. Vines do well on lower, south facing slopes, and do not mind poor soil. The valleys round Turin and the upper Rhone produce many famous wines.

Some wines of much less distinction are produced in higher areas, and these are turned into brandy (Grappa in Italy) or vermouths, like Cinzano.

Turin is known as the vermouth capital. Many of these drinks, like Genepi di Alpi, are seasoned with Alpine herbs. One speciality from the Susa and Biella valleys is flavoured with rose petals and supposedly dates back to the Crusades. Critical wine experts say that making vermouth is the only way to make bad wine drinkable!

Alpine crops

Many crops will not grow well in the mountains – the soil is too poor, or the land too high for them. However, most valleys have some flat land and it is here that cereal crops, wheat, barley and oats, can be grown along with vegetables and fruit. Some valleys, like Sion in Switzerland, specialise in fruit and vegetables. Individual farmers no longer have to grow all the cereals and vegetables they need, as they are seldom cut off from supplies in winter as they used to be.

The main business of every farmer is to grow hay for winter feed. In some areas maize is also an important fodder crop. Some is cut green and fed to the animals right away. The rest is dried and stored hanging under the eaves of a barn for use in winter.

In parts of Italy and Bulgaria, coarse ground maize porridge is a popular food for people. In Italy this dish is known as polenta, and the people who eat it as polentas. Every year at Monastero Bormida in Italy, on the first Sunday in March, there is

a festival, called the Sagra di Polentonissimo. Huge piles of polenta are eaten by everyone, with lots of wine, to celebrate gifts of maize flour, given to the starving population by the Marquis Della Rovere at the end of the terrible winter of 1573.

North-south, east-west

What any valley will grow depends a great deal on its aspect. The south facing, northern slope of an east-west valley very often has all the houses and fields of a village on it. The north facing slope, which receives very little sun even in summer, grows only trees. In valleys which run north south, both sides can be farmed, as long as there is flat land.

Opposite page, above left: *Vines on the Route de Vignoble in the Sion Valley, Switzerland.* **Above right:** *Picking grapes to make wine. While some mountain areas produce good quality wines, less good wine is made into vermouth.* **Left:** *A mechanised hay rake, specially adapted to work on steeper slopes, arranges the hay into rows after it has been cut.*

Top right: *On some mountain farms hay and straw are still tied into traditional stooks to dry.* **Above:** *2,000 year old rice terraces cut into a mountainside at Banawe in the Philippines.* **Right:** *Maize drying under the wide eaves of a Swiss farm house. Maize was once a staple food for mountain people. Now it is usually used for animal feed.*

From farm to market

In the past when villages were quite isolated, farmers were dependent on their animals to provide all their basic needs. Even a small herd of cattle provided milk, cheese, butter and meat for the family. Sheep provided wool.

Modern transport has revolutionised mountain farming. People no longer practise **subsistence farming** (growing all they need). Now they are part of a much larger market of producers and consumers, growing **cash crops.**

Most mountain farmers still produce their own milk, butter and meat, but nowadays they also specialise, and sell their surpluses at local markets.

Smaller villages have one end-of-summer market, called a fiera in Italy. Larger ones hold a market day once a week. Cities have wholesale markets, like the enormous cattle market at Chivasso, which serves the whole region of Piedmont, in Italy.

Travelling traders buy animals in the villages and take them for sale in the valley towns.

There is also a system for marketing milk produced in the mountains. Farmers store their milk in stainless steel, cooled tanks, from which dairy lorries collect every few days. In some communities, especially in Switzerland, plastic pipelines connect the milking huts with the farmhouse.

Cheese is no longer simply for local consumption. The dairies sell famous cheeses like Emmenthal and Gruyère all over the world.

Old ewes are sold for mutton, while the main flock grazes on the alp in summer.

Goats are kept for milk to make cheeses.

Pigs are fattened on skimmed milk.

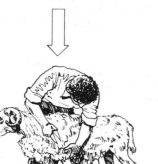

Heifers, young breeding cows, go up to the alps with the main herd.

Gangs of sheep shearers travel round villages in June and July.

Male calves (bullocks) are sold for veal in the spring.

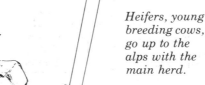

Milk is taken from the farms in tanker trucks to dairy factories.

Pigs are slaughtered in the autumn for hams, sausages, smoked meats and other specialities, as well as pork and bacon.

Male lambs are sold in spring to be fattened on lowland farms, or sent direct to market.

Meat is produced at large-scale abattoirs, near the cities where most of it is consumed.

Large dairies produce various cheeses. They also make yoghurts and other dairy products.

Things to do

1. WHAT HAVE YOU LEARNT?

Junior

a) *Nomads are people who:*
  – live permanently in one place ☐
  – wander aimlessly from place to place ☐
  – move around on a regular pattern seeking pasture ☐

b) *Seasonal migration from one region to another is:*
  – transalpine ☐
  – transhumance ☐
  – subsistence ☐

c) *Cattle have to be kept indoors for six months of the year because;*
  – the winter weather has become more severe ☐
  – modern transport enables them to be moved to summer pastures earlier in the year than before ☐
  – it is too cold in winter and there is no grazing outside ☐

d) *Flat land is provided on steep slopes by:*
  – terracing ☐
  – bulldozing ☐
  – landscaping ☐

Intermediate

a) *Mountain farmers are mainly pastoralists because:*
  – the ground is too steep to grow crops ☐
  – the climate only allows a short growing season ☐
  – animals fit into the mountain farming system better than crops ☐

b) *The main purpose of growing crops in mountain regions is:*
  – to feed the animals in winter ☐
  – to give the farmers something to do in summer ☐
  – to provide food for the family ☐

c) *The isolation of mountain farming communities has been broken by:*
  – modern means of communication ☐
  – large-scale government intervention ☐
  – travelling traders ☐

d) *It is usual to find a hierarchy of markets where:*
  – the small villages hold markets most frequently ☐
  – the largest towns hold annual markets ☐
  – the wholesale markets in the cities are open daily ☐

Advanced

a) *Symbiosis is:*
  – the interdependence of primitive herders and their flocks ☐
  – a modern dance craze ☐
  – the annual migration to summer grazings ☐

b) *Transhumance is a traditional form of adaptation to the mountain environment because:*
  – it makes efficient use of the available land ☐
  – it employs people at slack times ☐
  – it represents a conscious community decision ☐

c) *The EEC and governments are investing in mountain farming to:*
  – get the highest possible return on their money ☐
  – assist the rationalisation of mountain agriculture ☐
  – speed up rural depopulation ☐

d) *The solutions to the problems of mountain farming include:*
  – farmers taking other part-time jobs ☐
  – farmers staying bachelors ☐
  – increasing specialisation ☐

2. MOUNTAIN FARMERS

Until relatively recently many mountain farmers only produced enough to feed themselves and their families. Their agricultural system is illustrated in the diagram.

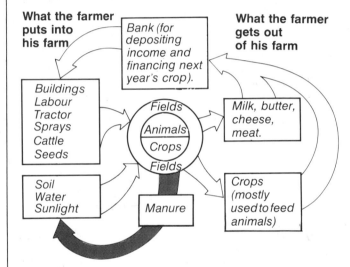

Junior

a) What does the mountain farmer put into (**inputs**) his farm?

b) What does the farmer get out (**outputs**) of his farm as a result of his inputs?

Intermediate

a) Why does the mountain farmer only have a limited range of inputs?

a) Why is the range of products limited?

Advanced

Redraw the farming system diagram to show the impact of government and private investment, tourism and the other agricultural reforms. What effect do they have on the inputs and outputs?

3. PROJECT – THE FARMER'S YEAR

Draw a circle and divide it into twelve equal parts, like a clock face. Starting at 12 o'clock, call the first division January. Write the name of all the months around the circle, then describe the farmer's work in each month throughout the year. When is he busiest and why? When is he least busy and why?

VI. Mountain settlements

Steep, high and cold places do not encourage human habitation. Their **steepness** makes them awkward to farm; the **altitude** can make people sick; and the **cold** makes it difficult to raise crops, or even to keep warm. So in temperate climates, the higher the mountains the smaller the population. In Switzerland five per cent of the population live above 1,000m (3,250ft) and only 0.5 per cent live above 1,500m (5,000ft)

In hot places, however, the position is reversed. People take refuge from the heat of the plains by going to the cool mountains. In Colombia, South America, 98 per cent of the population live in the Andean areas.

Apart from the physical conditions, there are several reasons why people may choose to live in mountain regions. Some groups have been persecuted, as cultural and religious minorities for example, and taken to the hills for refuge. Other mountain settlements are strategically placed to defend frontiers, like the fortress town of Briançon in France.

The vast majority of mountain settlements were not planned. They were established because they offered people some advantage in their situation. Certain places would obviously not attract people as good village sites – on a marshy valley floor, given to flooding, in the path of avalanches, or in permanent shade.

Good locations

Other spots would be much more suitable – where there was **good soil**, a **water supply** but **no flood danger**, **level**, open, **sunny land** good for farming. Another site might have good **defence** possibilities. It might be well placed for **trading**, or at a **river crossing**, or any combination of advantages.

While it is true that, in temperate regions, people tend to avoid living in the mountains, it is also certain that they tend to cluster together at the foot of the mountains. The alluvial soil in the lower valleys is very often fertile. There are springs to provide plentiful clean water. Some of these springs, like those at Evian, have become the basis of a large mineral water industry. The flat land in the valley bottom can be used for industry,

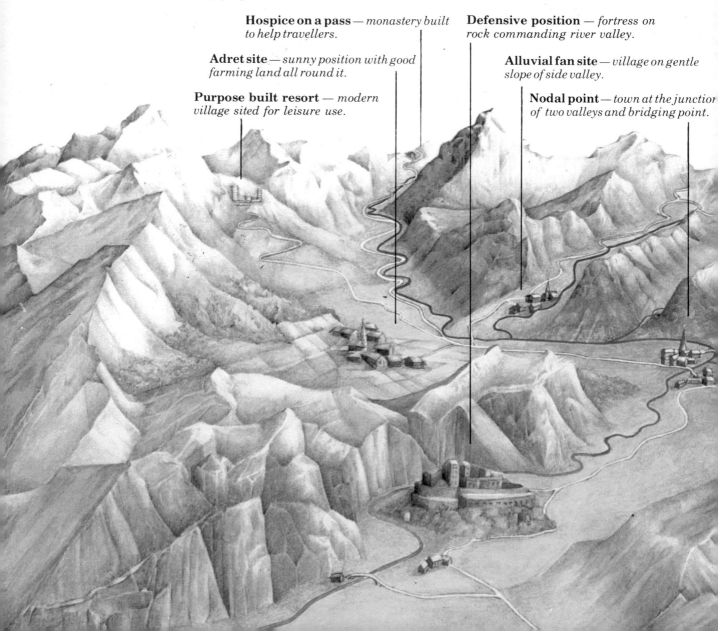

Hospice on a pass — *monastery built to help travellers.*

Adret site — *sunny position with good farming land all round it.*

Purpose built resort — *modern village sited for leisure use.*

Defensive position — *fortress on rock commanding river valley.*

Alluvial fan site — *village on gentle slope of side valley.*

Nodal point — *town at the junction of two valleys and bridging point.*

powered by hydro-electricity. Some valley towns were established as staging posts. Places like Susa and Bolzano were the last towns travellers could reach by conventional transport, like carriages. For the journey over the pass they used horses or mules.

On a journey up a mountain valley today it is possible to see examples of towns and villages formed for many of these reasons.

A large town like Trento in Italy, is usually to be found at a **nodal point**, where two valleys meet. Further up there might be a **river crossing** town, like Bormio. Along the sides of glacially gouged valleys, there are often villages built on **talus cones**, or **alluvial fans** of good soil washed down from a side valley. At a narrow defile,

there might be a **castle,** like Exilles between Suza and Sauze d'Oulx. Other villages are sited on the flat **terraces** of gravel above the river bank, out of the way of floods. Yet others, like Lauterbrunnen in Switzerland, are **linear villages,** strung out along the banks of a stream.

Warmth and water are two of the most important factors affecting mountain settlements. Where possible villages tend to be on the sunny, adret side of a valley. In the upper Valais 86 per cent of the people live on the adret. Mountains can be dry places at certain times of the year, so a reliable spring or stream is needed, often to irrigate hay crops. In the Estrela mountains of central Portugal, there are only three months without frost,

and two of them are certain to be without rain.

Purpose built villages

Finally, there are some mountain settlements that obey none of the rules, because man has built them for a special purpose. Sestriere in Italy and Isola in France were specially built as ski resorts, far higher than traditional villages. France has many purpose-built ski resorts. Some have been built in a futuristic style. In other places an industrial project like a mine or a dam necessitates a small settlement. Highest of all in the Alps, are the ancient hospices, like the St Bernard, where the monks and their dogs have been helping travellers for hundreds of years.

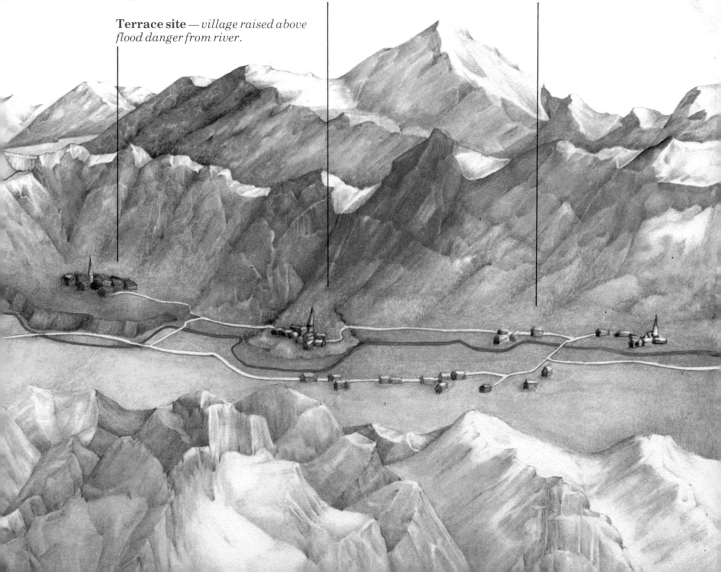

Industrial site — *a few houses for hydro-electric station staff.*

Terrace site — *village raised above flood danger from river.*

Talus cone site — *Village on cone of debris fallen from valley wall.*

Linear village — *houses strung out along flat valley floor near river.*

Alpine houses

The style and construction of a house depends on two things: the needs of the people who are going to live in it and the materials available for building. If the people are prosperous, they may add another element, decoration.

There is no such thing as a typical **Alpine chalet.** But there are some characteristics, which most of them have. Because of the symbiotic relationship between the mountain farmer and his animals, most houses are built for both of them. The farmer must also store, in the same house or a separate barn, his hay and his grain. Alpine houses are built for maximum protection against the winter snow and cold. They mostly have steep roofs, so the snow slides off, with wide eaves, under which wood can be stored. They are solidly built to retain whatever warmth is available, from a wood fire or from the animals.

Varieties of style

The style and construction of Alpine houses varies from north to south. In general in the north, the Chablais region in France, the Valais in Switzerland and the Tyrol in Austria, houses are built of **wood** on a stone foundation. Through the central part of the Alps, they are **half wood half stone.** And in the south, mostly in Italy, they are entirely **stone.**

This is a result of both the availability of materials and local custom. In the Italian speaking Ticino canton of Switzerland, houses are built of stone, as they are further south. The German speaking Walser minority around Macugnaga in Italy brought their wooden building style with them from the north.

The houses of Alpine villages tend to be clustered together. There is very little fertile land, so as little of it as possible was used for buildings. People had to be near the **communal well,** and sometimes there was a communal oven also, to save fuel. Having houses close together was useful in bad weather, especially in a winter emergency. Most houses were built into the side of a hill, facing the valley and if possible facing south.

Accommodation

Houses built mainly on one floor, like those in the Haut Chablais in France, had a covered hallway called a **cortena.** This entrance led into the barn on one side and the house on the other. The human accommodation consisted of a kitchen called the **outa.** This was also the summer sitting room. Further on there was a living room called the **pele.** This had an enormous chimney at one end. The fire was the centre of life throughout the winter. People sat round it, practising winter crafts, like weaving and carving. Hams and sausages were hung inside it to smoke. The bedrooms were either alcoves off the kitchen and living room, or small separate rooms. The **barn** next door consisted of stalls for the cows, sheep, goats and pigs and perches for the hens. Hay and grain were kept in the roof or in a separate store house nearby.

In other areas mountain chalets were larger and built on several stories. Some were very large and owned by two families. There are still houses like this to be seen in the Bernese Oberland and Engadine valley in Switzerland. A typical multistory house had a barn for the animals on the ground floor. The people lived on the first floor (the heat from the animals rising from below), and the hay was stored in the roof space. As the house would have been built into the side of a hill, it was possible to load the hay and grain directly into the loft from a cart on a ramp at the back.

Exterior decoration

Like the construction of Alpine houses, the styles of exterior decoration varied from region to region. The wooden houses of the north had beautifully **carved beams** and **balustrades.** Ventilation holes were made in stylish designs – hearts, clubs and crosses were popular in Savoy in France. Further south there was less decoration, although some houses in Italy have intricate **religious murals** on them.

Left: *Animal central heating. In the French Alps, and other areas, animals occupied part of the house. Warmth from the sheep warmed the alcove bed. The sheep could be fed without going outside, by lifting the bench seat.*
Below left: *This typical house in Savoy, France, was divided into two, the left hand part occupied by the farmer's family and the right hand side by cows, pigs, chickens and the hay store.*
Below: *Typical Swiss chalet, built into the side of the hill.*

Plan of typical French Alpine house.

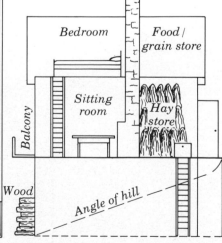

Cross section of house on a slope.

Above: *Typical mural, Italian Alps.* **Below:** *Stone house with balcony, and wood stored under it.*

Above: *Villages like Lajetto, Italy, were built clustered together.* **Below:** *Rough stone construction in Lajetto. Thatch is now rare. On the next page there is a plan of the village.*

Left: *A typical wooden house in the Bernese Oberland, Switzerland.* **Below:** *House in the Auvergne, France, Beds are in alcoves on the left, with a door into the scullery beyond. The fire place was the centre of life all winter.*

Depopulation and development

Until recently mountain dwellers faced lives of great hardship, and sometimes even famine. As a result they have always taken every opportunity to escape their harsh environment. It is only since skiing became popular that prosperity has come to many Alpine villages.

Tough mountain conditions bred tough men. In the middle ages the Swiss peasants were Europe's soldiers of fortune. The Swiss Guards at the Vatican are the remnants of a seventeenth century mercenary army. In the British Army, the Scots Highland brigades are still notorious for their ferocity.

Large scale emigration

In the nineteenth century large numbers of people emigrated from Europe's mountain areas, both to the colonies and the newly industrialised towns. Statistics show that in Britain the **de-population** of highland regions began seriously in the early 1800s. In France this trend began in the 1840s and in Italy and Austria it began in the 1890s. In Austria there was a temporary increase in mountain population during the difficult period that followed the First World War. In the last 100 years 50 per cent of the population of France's mountain areas has left – sometimes with curious results. The town of Barcelonnette boasts many luxurious mansions, all built with fortunes made by local people in the textile trade in Mexico.

Many Scandinavians and Swiss went to America. Wisconsin is not a mountainous area, but it specialises in dairy produce and is called the Switzerland of America. Rivers like the Fraser and MacKenzie in Canada bear the names of hardy Scots explorers. The Welsh established a settlement in Patagonia, where Welsh is still spoken.

Many Italians emigrated to the USA and Australia, or to the factories in Turin and Milan. Locana, near the Gran Paradiso National Park, had a population of 8,000 in 1900, but today it has only 1,500 people.

Mountain metropolis

For almost 700 years the village of Chamonix was poor, isolated and independent, ruled by the Prior of a monastery. Situated at the foot of Mont Blanc, the highest mountain in the Alps, it was one of the first places visited by tourists, who came mostly from England. The **first hotel**, built in 1770 was called the Hotel d'Angleterre. In 1866 a **new road** was built up to Chamonix and the tourist business boomed. In 1901 the **railway** reached Chamonix, and soon after winter sports began in earnest. In 1965 the **Mont Blanc Tunnel** was opened and the town developed again, as it will yet again when the autoroute from Geneva reaches it in 1981. Chamonix is now a metropolis of the mountains, but in a less spectacular way its development is paralleled by that of every small ski resort.

Development has brought many advantages to mountain people. Villagers use the shops, the electricity and water supplies put in to serve tourists. Hotels employ local people.

Some forms of development are better for villagers than others. The large blocks of flats to be seen in many Italian resorts are now being discouraged. Statistics show that one extra job is created for every 6-12 hotel beds in a resort, while it takes 60-80 apartment beds to create a new job.

While development makes life better for poor people, it is not always as welcome as it might seem. Mountain settlements were often close, old-fashioned societies, and many people have resented the end of their traditional customs and life.

Above: *Life in mountain villages used to be very harsh. Many people moved to cities.* **Right:** *Today new villages like Isola, France, are built for skiers.*

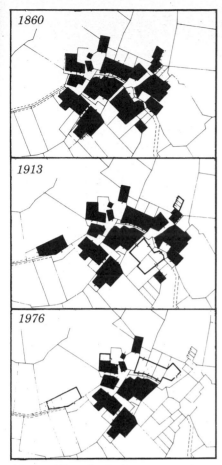

1860

1913

1976

Above: *How the Italian mountain village of Lajetto lost its people. The black areas indicate houses that were occupied.* **Right:** *Chamonix today.* **Below right:** *Chamonix in its early days as a resort, mid-1800s.* **Below left:** *Railway poster advertising Chamonix.*

SPORTS D'HIVER
AU COL DE VOZA PAR St GERVAIS
CHEMIN DE FER DU MONT-BLANC

ROGER BRODERS

Village and outside world

Modern transport and communications, tourism and industry ensure that the life of every mountain village is closely linked to life in other, larger places. These may be towns down the valley, and even cities hundreds of miles away. There is a **hierarchy of towns** and villages rather like the hierarchy of a school, starting with a board of governors, then the headmaster, the heads of departments, the senior students, right down to the newest pupil.

There are different **hierarchies** for different aspects of life – government, law, medicine, industry, tourism and trade are a few of them. The mountain village is almost always at the end of the line, but is is not necessarily the most unimportant place. The tourists on whom its economy depends, may need the organisation provided by Milan airport, a bus company from Sondrio, and a travel company in England. But their destination is say, Madesimo, and that is the important place to them. That is also the most important place as far as the Italian economy is concerned. Tourists come to ski, not to visit Milan airport, or go by bus to Sondrio.

Regional government
Every country has its own form of **local government**. In England the basic unit of local government is the **county,** in Germany it is the **Land,** in France the **département,** in Switzerland the **canton** and in Italy the **regione.** These organisations are in the middle of the hierarchy, between the **national government** and the **village**. But as far as mountain areas are concerned it is the regione, in Italy for example, that is the most important.

The regione of Piemonte has a **giunta,** or council of local MPs who represent the different parts of an area that is 150km (110 miles) wide and 250km (150 miles) long. The MPs meet in the regional capital, Turin. There they are assisted by a local bureaucracy, divided into four departments, each of which has many sub-departments, called **assessorati.** One of these is the **Assessorato alla Montagna,** which deals with all the problems particular to the mountains. Another is the **Assessorato al Turismo.**

Below the regional government is the provincial government and then the village, with its **mayor,** or **sindaco.** Again because of the special problems of the mountain environment, there is another organisation recently created, the **comunità montana.** This represents the interests of a whole valley, coordinating projects and wielding more influence than one village can manage on its own. Each village sends three representatives, two of the majority and one of the opposition. The physical geography of Piedmont shows that there are a number of large valleys all leading down to the Po plain. Each one has its own comunità, except the Valley of Susa, which has two because it is very large. Alta (Upper) Susa consists of places like Oulx, Exilles, Claviere, Bardonecchia and Sestriere, which are farming and ski villages. Bassa (Lower) Valle di Susa is an industrial area that runs almost to Turin. Oulx is the administration centre for both comunità. Thus the government hierarchy runs from the village, like Sauze d'Oulx or Bardonecchia, Oulx and the comunità, to the regional government in Turin, and finally to the national government in Rome.

Hierarchies in everything
Other facets of life have similar hierarchies. Small village shops often sell mainly food. For large items, like washing machines, a trip to the nearest town may be necessary. In Sauze d'Oulx there is a doctor specialising in ski injuries. There is a medium-sized hospital in Susa, but all serious cases go to Turin. In Sauze d'Oulx there is a garage, but for car parts and major service it is necessary to go down to the valley. In the lower Susa valley there are many industries, including steel, employing people from the higher valleys, and providing goods and services for the area. The attractions of Turin are not far away. Many people commute to work in factories like Fiat.

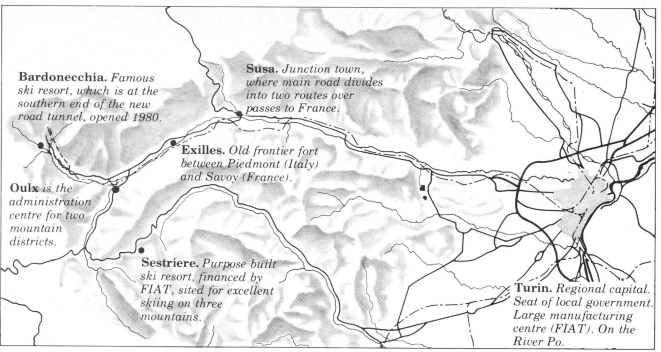

Bardonecchia. *Famous ski resort, which is at the southern end of the new road tunnel, opened 1980.*

Susa. *Junction town, where main road divides into two routes over passes to France.*

Exilles. *Old frontier fort between Piedmont (Italy) and Savoy (France).*

Oulx *is the administration centre for two mountain districts.*

Sestriere. *Purpose built ski resort, financed by FIAT, sited for excellent skiing on three mountains.*

Turin. *Regional capital. Seat of local government. Large manufacturing centre (FIAT). On the River Po.*

Above: *Map of the upper and lower Susa Valley, showing the hierarchy of towns and villages from the regional capital, Turin, to resorts like Bardonecchia.*

Below: *The fortress of Exilles guarded the French-Italian frontier on the Dora Riparia river.* **Left:** *Susa is an important centre for nearby mountain villages.*

Left: *An aerial view of Turin, the capital of Piedmont and seat of regional government.* **Right:** *Bardonecchia, a ski resort. These two places are at opposite ends of the settlement hierarchy.*

Resorts in winter and summer

In the nineteenth century people began to visit the Alps, mainly in summer, to rest in the clean, crisp air – a real change from the sooty and smog-bound atmospheres of cities like London. Tuberculosis was a killer disease and sufferers went to sanitoria at high altitude in search of a cure.

Many mountain villages also boasted mineral water springs, to which people came from all over Europe. Many spa towns, Vichy in France and Baden-Baden in Germany for example, still attract people to take a cure. St Moritz, now one of the most fashionable of all ski resorts, first became famous for its waters, supposed to be good for the liver. Bormio, in Italy, was a Roman spa town.

By the end of the last century, tourists had begun to visit the Alps for winter sports, which have been developing ever since. Switzerland now has over 100 ski resorts, 185 ski schools and receives over half a million winter visitors each year. 100,000 of them are British. Italy has over 130 resorts in the Alps alone, and others all over the country, including one on Mt Etna in Sicily.

Nordic and Alpine skiing

Traditionally skiing is divided into two disciplines – Nordic and Alpine. **Nordic skiing,** as its name suggests, comes from Scandinavia and includes ski jumping and cross-country skiing. Ski de Fond (French) Ski di Fondo (Italian) and Langlauf (German), as cross-country skiing is known, is the original form of the sport. It has made a come back recently, and now most resorts have marked tracks for this form of hiking on special skis.

Alpine skiing, also called downhill skiing, is by the far the most popular winter sport. In the Alps the season begins before Christmas and lasts until late April. At some very high resorts, like Tignes in France, it is possible to ski 365 days a year.

There are many variations of skiing. From America comes an exuberant and dare-devil variety, called freestyle. This involves acrobatics, spins and somersaults. Ski ballet is gaining favour, and there is a contest known as mogul-bashing for those who like a rough ride! Those who wish to combine tobogganing with skiing, ride ski-bobs. Lifts at many resorts have special hooks for them.

After skiing, skating is probably the most popular winter sport, together with other ice-rink events, like ice hockey and curling, a form of bowls on ice.

Summer activities

Since tourism has become the major source of income for many mountain villages, most have developed some summer attractions to fill hotels in the off season. Hiking, fishing, boating on lakes, tennis, riding, swimming and just enjoying the scenery are some of the holiday activities possible in the mountains.

Below: *Cross-country skiing is gaining popularity all over Europe.*

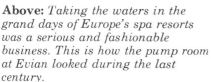

Above: *Taking the waters in the grand days of Europe's spa resorts was a serious and fashionable business. This is how the pump room at Evian looked during the last century.*

Above centre: *Some ski resorts now attract many summer tourists, especially to play tennis.*

Above right: *Some of the lower mountain areas provide good riding facilities.*

Right: *Fresh air and exercise are among the major attractions of the mountains. Hiking has become an extremely popular pastime for city dwellers.*

Below: *Freestyle skiing started in America, but now competitions are held all over the world.*

Below right: *Mountains are ideal for sports like hang-gliding.*

VII. Food processing

The people of a region like the Alps, under snow for half the year, did not have the luxury of eating fresh food all the time. They had to preserve their spring and summer surpluses for winter use. The modern equivalent of this past necessity is the food processing industry, which today exports mountain products all over the world.

Grass as a crop

Good grass is the most important crop produced in mountainous areas. It is cut and dried to be fed to animals in winter. In spring and summer it feeds the main producers of food – the cows, goats and sheep.

Cows calve in spring, when the grass is richest. They produce milk, because they have borne calves – not because they eat grass! The new grass encourages milk production to such an extent that there is more than the farmer can use. But as milk does not keep for more than a few days, there is a limit to how much of it can be sold fresh. Most of it must be made into something that will not go bad so quickly. If milk is made into other products, like **butter, cheese, yoghurt,** and even **chocolates** (for which Switzerland is famous), it can be sold in much wider markets, and all the year round. In addition, the factories that make milk products employ local people, and bring another source of income to the region.

The grass that feeds the cows, also fattens the calves, which are sold for meat. The traditional mountain farmer had to make the meat that he kept for himself into a form that would last the winter, just as he made cheeses to eat when no milk was being produced.

His solution to the problem of preserving meat was to smoke it. The huge fireplaces that were the centre of family life also served to smoke hams and sausages. The mountain delicacies of jambon cru in France and prosciutto in Italy are uncooked, **smoked hams** originally made by farmers for winter.

In some places legs of mutton, beef, and goat are cured in the same way. Smaller pieces of meat, or offal, were made into sausages. The **saucisson** of France and the **salami** of Italy are now world famous. They are very often made of hard-packed minced pork, with strong seasonings, made up into sausages 30-40cms (about 1ft) long and 6-8cms (3ins) in diameter.

Factory production

Today most meat and milk products are made in factories. The town of St Gervais, near Chamonix, France, has given its name to a whole brand range of milk products. The cheese factory at Gruyères, in Switzerland, processes over 13,000 litres (3,000 gallons) of milk , making about 1,200kg (over 1 tonne) of cheese, a day.

The cheese is made in a copper vat. Rennet is added to the warmed milk, to make it curdle. The curdled mass separates into whey and cheese grains, as it is heated to 55℃ (130℉). The mixture is then run off into pressing pans. The whey is squeezed out under pressure, and siphoned off to be made into animal feed. The cheeses are then put into a salt bath to form the rind. They then mature in storage for about three months.

Water and wine

Not all mountain products are made from milk. Vines grow well on some mountain slopes. The upper Rhone valley, near Leysin, Switzerland, the Dora Riparia valley around Susa and the Valtellina and Adige valleys in Italy are all famous **wine** producing areas. In winter the vines are nothing more than dormant stumps. But in spring they shoot new growth, and the grapes are harvested in autumn. There are now many factory products made from mountain grapes – herbs are added to some wines to make **vermouths,** while some grapes are made into a form of Brandy called **eau-de-vie** in France, or **grappa** in Italy.

As we take good water for granted, it seems strange that a major industry should grow up bottling mountain **spring water** for sale all over the world. But this is just what has happened in many places, like Evian on the south side of Lake Geneva. Evian was a spa town in the last century. But today its main industry is Evian water. This comes from springs fed from snow high in the mountains. Geologists reckon that it takes 15 years for the water to filter through beds of glacial sand to the spring. As a result it is very pure when it emerges. It is piped directly from the spring to the bottling plant, where it is checked in over 200 tests a day. Amazingly enough the mineral content of the water has not changed since the first analysis was carried out in 1807.

Above: *Nineteenth century water bottling methods at Evian. The water has been sold since 1807.*

Above: *Today Evian comes in plastic bottles. It is analysed for purity over 200 times a day.*

Above: *In a dairy milk is warmed to make it curdle.* **Top right:** *Making chocolates in a Swiss factory.* **Right:** *Stamping Emmental cheese during its three-month maturing period.* **Below:** *Smoking hams in Austria.*

Fondue

Traditional mountain dish. There are two kinds of fondue – meat and cheese. A **meat fondue** is made by spearing individual lumps of beef onto a long fork and cooking it in boiling oil. A **cheese fondue** is more complicated.

Here is a **recipe** for it. For every person you need: 220g (8 oz) of Swiss cheese; 1 cup of dry white wine; 1 tablespoon of potato flour; 1 small glass of kirsch; 1 clove of garlic; half a loaf of bread, cut into cubes; a pinch of black pepper.

Method: Smear the inside of a fireproof dish with garlic; grate cheese into the dish with wine; stir the mixture over an alcohol burner;

add pepper; dissolve flour in kirsch; add to mixture gradually, keeping it simmering; cook and stir for 15 mins, until smooth. Spear bread with forks and dip into fondue.

Power for industry

Three ingredients are necessary to the establishment of industry – raw materials, skilled labour and capital. Investment money can be moved round the world with relative ease, but it is harder to bring together the people and the raw materials.

The mountains of Europe have always produced skilled artisans, both men and women. During the enforced leisure of winter they wove textiles and worked wood or metal to supplement their incomes. In Roman times there were a few raw materials mined in the Alps and the Piedmontese were known as skilled metal workers.

But the Alps lacked major resources until, about 100 years ago, it was discovered that electricity could be made by water power. Following Britain's industrial revolution lead, there had been attempts to set up textile factories using water power, in Piedmont in the 1700s. But it was **hydro-electricity** that brought large scale industry to the Alps. White oil, as it is known, transformed whole regions near the mountains. The Swiss have equipped themselves with hydro power to such an extent that they now produce four per cent of the entire world's output.

New industry

Some of these new electricity-based industries exploited existing resources that were almost useless without power. A water powered paper mill existed at Caselle, near Turin in 1181. There had always been forests nearby to produce the wood, and there was plenty of clean water, also essential to paper making. But suddenly it was possible to make **pulp** and **paper** on a large scale and today there are several major mills in Piedmont, like the Burgo factory at Verzuolo, near Cuneo. There had always been **quarries** in the mountains. But now electric pulverisers could be used to make **cement** and **aggregates**. Power could be used to churn **butter** and separate **cheese** on an industrial, instead of a farmhouse, scale.

Traditional skills like weaving and sewing could be mechanised. A small silk industry in 1900 has become the modern **textile manufacturing** centre of Biella.

Other industries were entirely new. The production of hydro-electricity itself became an industry – building dams and power stations and running them. Of the 1500 people who live in the Locana valley, 360 are electricity supply workers. Today huge dams, like Tignes and Mont Cenis, supply the industrial areas of Lyon and St Etienne, as well as the French Riviera, with power.

Electro-metallurgy, processing metals by electricity, requires enormous amounts of cheap power, usually only available from water. The St Jean de Maurienne aluminium smelter was built in the Arc river valley in

Above: *Old-fashioned water-power.*
Right: *Dams and hydro-electricity have brought industry to the Alps.*

1907 and it expanded rapidly. By World War II it was one of the biggest factories in south-east France. Availability of power is still the most important factor in making aluminium. The smelter at Bluff in New Zealand is powered by electricity from the lakes of the Southern Alps. Current expansion programmes will probably make it one of the largest in the world. Other metal processing industries have come to valleys like the Arc in Savoy, France. Special steels, like alloys of tungsten (light-weight strength for aircraft) and chromium (stainless steel) are made in electric furnaces. Much of the **chem-ical industry** depends on the process of electrolysis. Nitric acid is made by fixing nitrogen under an electric arc, for example. Large chemical plants, too, are to be found in the Arc valley.

Italy's industrial belt

The combination of cheap power and local steel supplies encouraged other industries. The first **cars** built in Turin were made by Michele Lancia in 1895. Fiat was formed in 1899. Today the company employs over 200,000 people, making 1.6 million cars a year as well as tractors, trucks, jet aircraft, and marine engines, among other things. The first stage of industrialisation of the nothern Italian plain took place during the early years of this century. But it is since 1945 that it has developed so spectacularly. The industrial belt now stretches from the Olivetti factories at Ivrea, at the foot of the mountains in the west, to the oil refineries at Mestre, near Venice, in the east.

Below: *Quarry at Bellegarde, near the French-Swiss border. Gravels deposited by a glacier make excellent roadstone.* **Bottom:** *The Rhone Poulenc petro-chemical complex at Pont de Claix, France.*

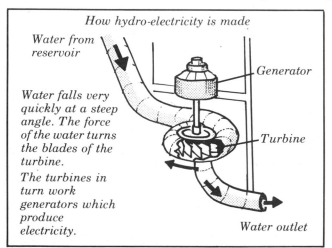

How hydro-electricity is made

Water from reservoir

Generator

Water falls very quickly at a steep angle. The force of the water turns the blades of the turbine.

Turbine

The turbines in turn work generators which produce electricity.

Water outlet

Managing the forests

The mountain foresters of Europe long ago discovered that conservation is good business. The Alpine regions have a long history of good forest management, making maximum use of the forest, while ensuring it continues to grow and produce timber. But this was not always the case.

Timber is a renewable resource. Unlike coal and oil, which once they have been burnt are gone for ever, forests can be regrown in a relatively short period – 30 to 150 years according to the type of tree. But forests can also be destroyed very easily by over-exploitation – cutting trees regardless of the future of the forest. This is what happened in Europe for hundreds of years. It is still happening to a certain extent in North America, South America and the Far East, but gradually people all over the world are learning the lessons that the Alpine foresters learned at the end of the eighteenth century.

In most mountain regions, forest is the natural vegetation, up to a certain altitude. Land that is left entirely to itself will eventually produce what is called **climax vegetation** – the selection of trees and plants natural to the environment. In the lower foothills of the Alps this natural vegetation consists of **hardwoods**, like beech and oak. These are deciduous trees, which means that they loose their leaves in winter. Above the hardwoods grow the **conifers**, Norway spruce, silver fir and larch, the only deciduous conifer. All these trees grow in the Alps, but they have not always grown as thickly as they do today.

In France, which has little coal, wood was the chief source of heat for hundreds of years. Wood fires heated city houses; charcoal fired the iron foundaries of the early industrial revolution. The demands on the forests were enormous, but once the land had been cleared it was not replanted with trees, but used as pasture for expanding farms. By the middle of the nineteenth century France had less than half the forest it has today (8 million hectares, 19.75 million acres). Not only was there a shortage of wood, the hills that were once covered in trees were suffering terrible erosion. New laws were enacted, laying the basis for the careful management practices used today.

Three uses of forests

Forested land has three principal uses. Firstly the trees are valuable for **timber** and **timber products**. Larger logs are sold as saw timber, for use in building

and making furniture, for example. Less high quality wood, smaller logs and off-cuts are made into pulp for papermaking and packaging or made into chipboard.

Secondly trees play an important role in **protecting the environment**. They absorb carbon dioxide and put oxygen into the atmosphere. Their roots hold together the soil, preventing erosion, especially on steep slopes prone to land-slides. They also help to prevent floods, by slowing up the run-off of snow melt-water and heavy rainfall.

Thirdly, forests provide excellent **wildlife reserves** and **recreation areas**, popular with campers, hikers, cross-country skiers and naturalists. Forest land would not be able to perform these three valuable functions if it was not properly maintained.

Forest managers in the mountains of Europe practise a system of **selective management** and **felling** – growing trees in groups of mixed ages and only cutting those trees that have grown to maturity. Extracting the full grown trees from the dense forest is not easy and selective felling is not the most efficient way to cut trees. In North America it is still common practice to clear a whole hillside at a time, regardless of the size of the trees. This is a rapid and economic method, but the price has to be paid later, when the trees do not grow back and the mountainside is eroded. With selective felling it is often not necessary to replant, as the forest regenerates naturally.

Local industry

For most Alpine communities forestry and timber milling are important local industries. Many of the communities actually own the forest round them. In Italy 20 per cent of the land is under forest and 36 per cent of the forest is community owned. In Germany 29 per cent of the land is under forest, and 25 per cent of it owned by local villages. In France 25 per cent of land is forested and 20 per cent of it in community ownership.

Foresters, employed by the local authority, by the state forest services, or by private owners, cut the selected trees and haul them to the nearest road with a tractor and winch. Occasionally in large scale operations a cable hoist is used, or even a helicopter. The logs are then loaded onto a truck and taken to the sawmill. The saw-timber, cut from the logs, is dispatched by rail or road to far away markets, while the chips are sent to nearby paper mills.

Far left: *Selective felling in the French Jura. Cutting only the larger trees can be awkward in thick forest. One man cuts, trims and hauls the logs to nearby roads.*
Above left: *Large scale operations in Canada, felling a whole slope. This can lead to serious erosion.*
Below left: *Smaller logs are stacked ready for pulping at a Canadian paper mill.*
Right: *Logging trucks with up to 24 forward gears transport logs down to timber mills.*
Below: *A family run sawmill in the French Jura mountains.*
Below right: *Removing water from wood pulp during paper making in a Canadian mill.*

Things to do

1. WHAT HAVE YOU LEARNT?

Junior

a) *The most important crop in mountainous areas is:*
  – grass ☐
  – grapes ☐
  – barley ☐

b) *Spring water is:*
  – water drunk only in spring ☐
  – pure water bottled for sale ☐
  – water collected from mountain springs ☐

c) *White oil is:*
  – oil which has been dyed white ☐
  – a special type of clean oil ☐
  – hydro-electric power ☐

d) *A renewable resource is:*
  – one that can be used over and over again ☐
  – one that can be renewed in a relatively short time ☐
  – one that is finished as soon as it has been used ☐

Intermediate

a) *The rind around cheese is made by:*
  – placing the cheese in a salt bath ☐
  – adding rennet to the warmed milk ☐
  – allowing it to mature for three months ☐

b) *Heavy metallurgical industries are often found in mountain areas because:*
  – the metals are found in the rocks ☐
  – hydro-electric schemes provide cheap power ☐
  – there is a ready supply of labour ☐

c) *Forests serve an environmental as well as a commercial function by:*
  – enhancing the scenery ☐
  – supplying the atmosphere with carbon dioxide ☐
  – binding the soil and preventing rapid run-off of water ☐

d) *One of the problems faced by the mountain farmer was preserving his products over the long winter. He did it by:*
  – converting perishable products into long-life products ☐
  – buying refrigerators and freezers ☐
  – smoking them throughout the winter ☐

Advanced

a) *Food processing industries in mountain areas grew up:*
  – out of necessity ☐
  – because of the supply of raw materials ☐
  – as a result of the available pool of labour ☐

b) *Management of forests is essential to prevent:*
  – trespassing ☐
  – unlawful cutting ☐
  – overexploitation ☐

c) *Local forests have long been a bonus to inhabitants because:*
  – they provided a hiding place during wars ☐

  – they provided additional grazing for their cattle ☐
  – they provided the main source of heating and building materials ☐

d) *More countries do not invest in hydro-electric power because:*
  – it is not as efficient as coal or oil ☐
  – they do not have the necessary environmental conditions ☐
  – it is too expensive ☐

2. MANUFACTURING IN THE MOUNTAINS

Mountain regions often contain pockets of important manufacturing industries, which can rely on a cheap and reliable supply of power from hydro-electricity. Some countries, such as Switzerland and Norway, derive a large proportion of their energy needs from this source. As long as it keeps raining and snowing, these countries do not need to use much oil or coal to generate electricity.

Simplified cross section of the Val de Bagnes and Rhone Valley hydro-electric scheme

Junior
Look back at the diagram of how hydro-electricity is produced on page 65. Also study the diagram above.
a) Describe in your own words how water generates electricity?
b) Try to find out if Britain has any hydro-electric plants and where they are?

Intermediate
a) What are the natural advantages of mountains for producing hydro-electricity?
b) What is meant by a head of water?

Advanced
a) Why do more countries not turn to hydro-electricity as the source of their power, if it reduces or removes dependence on costly imported fuels, like oil or coal?

3. CHANGING WITH THE TIMES

Intermediate

Traditionally villages had their own dairies where the milk was made into butter and cheese for local use. Nowadays these have been closed and one larger central dairy receives all the milk from the villages over a wide area. The butter and cheese produced is marketed by cooperatives. Below is a diagram showing how this happened in one part of the Swiss Valais.

a) What advantages does this centralisation offer the small farmer?

b) How have the developments in transport and refrigeration helped these larger dairies?

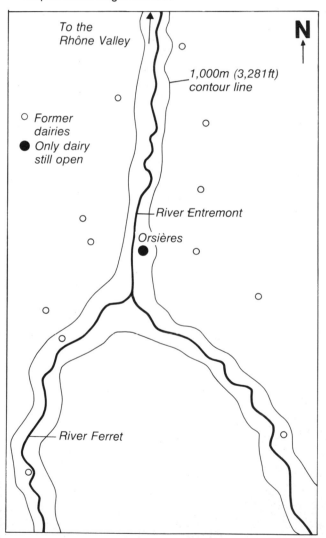

Advanced

Centralisation, rationalisation, amalgamation, cooperation and specialisation are five important methods of changing the agricultural system. Find out what each of these processes involves and how they effect farmers and their way of life. What are the most frequent results? Make a list of the advantages and disadvantages of each process.

4. THREATS TO THE FOREST

Junior

a) List four different ways in which a forest fire could start.

b) Why are forest fires in the mountains more difficult to put out than fires on flatter ground?

c) Find out how aeroplanes are used to put out forest fires in mountainous areas.

Intermediate

In recent years the number and size of forest fires in Canada have increased dramatically. Here are some official statistics:

1976 – area damaged 2,159,209 hectares

1980 – area damaged approximately 3,731,913 hectares.

a) Explain any connection there may be between tourism and such an increase in fire damage.

b) Provide as many other possible reasons as you can to explain this increase in the number and size of fires.

Advanced

a) In what ways could the establishment of a ski resort be damaging to local woodland?

b) What is meant by natural regeneration?

c) Find out about the work of the Forestry Commission in Britain? Why is this work necessary?

5. MAKING AND MARKETING CHEESE

Junior

Look at the photographs on page 63 and the one below. Can you see which part of the cheese making process they show. Draw a flow chart similar to the one on page 48 to show the different stages in cheese production and how it is marketed.

VIII. Transport in the mountains

It was the railway that first made remote mountain valleys accessible to everyone. Since then, amazing machines have been developed to make transport easier once in the mountains.

Cable cars are used to move everything from food for hotels to mineral ores from mines. The huge, fully automatic Black Angel cableway in Greenland transports 160 tonnes of ore an hour in 11 tonne buckets 24 hours a day. In Switzerland cable cars are a normal part of the transport system – official statistics suggest that every Swiss man, woman and child takes 50 cable car rides a year.

Chairlifts, serving winter skiers and summer sightseers, were first installed before World War II. Today they are often used for supplying mountain cafés as well as for moving people.

Tracked snow buses are also used in many places for ferrying people and supplies. Snow buses also take tourists for a close up view of the huge Columbia Ice Field in Canada.

Most well developed resorts use piste machines to compress new snow and flatten out the worst moguls (bumps). They also act as snowdozers, moving snow around.

Skidoos (motorcycles on skis) are

used for fun, racing and exploring remote mountain areas. In Canada and the USA they are used by farmers for checking cattle and even by Eskimos for hunting. Racing skidoos reach over 100mph.

At the other extreme, sleighs and sledges are still used in many places, from smart Swiss resorts, like Zermatt, to remote farms for delivering hay to the cows.

Right: *The latest cable cars can carry up to 220 people or heavy freight loads.* **Below:** *Piste machines have made ski run maintenance a routine matter in modern resorts.* **Below left:** *The mountain railway at Chamonix.* **Below top right:** *Sleighs are still used in some fashionable resorts.* **Below lower right:** *Chairlifts are just one of many uphill transport systems available for skiers.*

Transformation by transport

Looking down on the Alps from the window of a modern jet, it is not difficult to see what a formidable barrier the mountains presented to travellers of centuries past. Until the eighteenth century, people only crossed the Alps to make war or a pilgrimage. Such were the hardships of their journeys that few thought about the beauty of the scenery, far less contemplated climbing the mountains for pleasure.

In 1402 a monk, named Adam of Usk, had this to say about his crossing of the St Gotthard pass: "I was drawn in an ox-wagon half-dead with cold and my eyes blindfold lest I should see the danger of the pass." In 1739 Horace Walpole said of the Alps, "I hope I shall never see them again."

In the eighteenth century naturalists and geologists began to take an interest in the Alps. They came to investigate glaciers and rocks or to examine the flora and fauna. By the nineteenth century, the rich and educated had changed their views of mountains. Byron and Goethe both wrote about the beauty of the Alps and many British aristocrats doing the Grand Tour stopped to wonder at the Alpine landscape.

The coming of the railways

It was the building of railways that made possible the development of many remote mountain areas. At first railways brought only summer visitors – usually to take mineral waters. Some came as mountaineers, like Edward Whymper, who was the first man to climb the Matterhorn in 1865.

Gradually winter visits became fashionable too. In 1859, St Moritz boasted only 450 winter visitors; by 1910 this had leaped to 10,000. In 1880 a Curling Club was formed in St Moritz and in 1888 a Tobogganing Club. Skiing only became popular at the turn of the century.

The Swiss were enthusiastic mountain railway builders. The line at Lauterbrunnen (769m 2,522ft) climbs to Wengen (1.274m 4,178ft) and reaches the Eiger glacier at 2,320m (7,609ft) before disappearing into the tunnel beneath the Eiger. This train enabled some of the first ski tourists (on trips organised by Sir Henry Lunn, the first man to organise ski holidays) to make long runs on their enormous wooden skis.

The Jungfrau railway was built between 1896 and 1912 and is the highest railway in Europe. The terminus at Jungfraujoch is 3,454m (11,333ft) high, and the steepest gradient on the line is 1 in 4. Rack and pinion railways, which could negotiate formidable climbs were built in places where ordinary railways would not have been possible. Today Switzerland is criss-crossed with a railway network 5,750km (3,600 miles) long.

Post buses and tunnels

Areas remote from railways remained isolated until the invention of cars and the building of new roads. Between the world wars, the Swiss and Norwegians pioneered the idea of post buses. A regular bus service linked the more remote villages and market towns, carrying people, goods and mail.

Road tunnels have brought great improvements in mountain transport. Many passes are closed in winter because of snow, ice or avalanches. The Mont Blanc tunnel, opened in 1965, cuts 20 hours off the drive from Paris to Rome in winter. In September 1980 the longest road tunnel in the world, the St Gotthard, opened. It is 16.3km (10 miles 350 yards) long. It is from Germany to Italy. The new Mont Cenis tunnel was also opened in 1980.

Air transport

The arrival of chartered jet aircraft completes the present day picture of mountain development. Today, thousands of visitors land in jumbo jets and transfer, in fleets of buses along motorways, to resorts crowded with huge hotels. The scale of winter sport and mountain tourism has changed dramatically and all because of the changes in the means of transport.

Above: *The old Mont Cenis railway tunnel and the new Mont Cenis road tunnel, opened in 1980.*

Below: *Snowploughs make it possible to keep open mountain roads in winter weather.*

Above: *Hairpin bends on the St. Gotthard Pass, Switzerland.* **Below right:** *Construction work on the Italian side of the recently-opened Mont Cenis tunnel linking Italy and France.* **Below left:** *A post bus delivering mail in the Swiss mountains.*

Getting there

The journey time from London to Geneva is 20 hours by coach, or train, and only three hours by air, including one and a half hours for check in, customs and baggage reclaim.

Yet the time advantage of air travel can easily be lost as a result of bad weather. In winter, **delays** and **diversions** are frequent. **Ice, snow, fog** and **rain** can prevent planes from taking off or landing. Airports are equipped with sophisticated machinery to assist pilots to make safe landings in bad weather. But sometimes even this is not enough to keep up the schedule.

Fog is enemy number one as far as the airlines are concerned. When air cools rapidly, the moisture in it condenses forming a cloud at ground level. This is officially called fog when visibility is less than 1km (1,100yds).

Pollution can make fog worse. At Heathrow fog can be aggravated by north-east winds blowing smoke from London over the airport. Certain geographical features encourage the formation of fog. The mountains of northern Italy trap cold air in the valley of the River Po, causing fog even when the air above is clear.

The thickness of fog at airports is measured by light sensitive cells near the runway. Visibility of 600 – 800m is necessary for touch down; 200m for take off; at 50m or less the airport is usually closed. The captain of the aircraft has the responsibility of deciding whether to take off, land or divert.

Ice on the runway is obviously dangerous for aircraft, so special vehicles test the surface by simulating the braking action of a plane's wheels. If the surface is slippery it is sprayed with glycol. The salt used on roads would corrode the aluminium fuselage. Heated water and glycol are also used on the wings of stationary aircraft to prevent ice forming.

Even a heavy shower can disrupt landings and take offs. The concrete surface of the runway is grooved so the wheels can grip without skidding on puddles. Experts patrol the runways measuring the depth of water on them. This information is passed to the pilot, who decides if the anti-skid devices attached to each wheel can cope with it.

The same anti-skid devices help with landings on snow. However, snow is usually cleared first by fleets of snowploughs and snow blowers.

The captain of every aircraft is provided with impressive technical assistance to deal with bad weather conditions, but in the end he alone is responsible for all the souls (as they are known in airways jargon) on board.

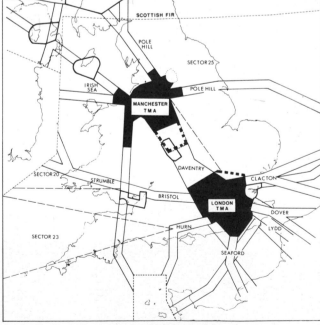

Left: *Testing the controls of a DC10.* **Top:** *Air Traffic Control Tower at Heathrow Airport, London. The Visual Control Room is at the top.* **Above:** *Aircraft must fly in airways, which are colour coded and numbered.*

Guide to Air Traffic Control

Air Traffic Control (ATC) exists to ensure the safe routine of airline flying all over the world. It depends on a network of highly trained air traffic controllers and their equipment.

Navigation Beacons guide aircraft in flight. After take off the pilot tunes in to the radio signal of the first beacon on his route. When he passes over it he homes in to the next, and so on.

A Flight Plan must be filed before departure by the pilot. He must take into consideration the weather, his route, target and speed, his fuel requirements and his estimated time of arrival (ETA). He must submit his flight plan to ATC.

A Progress Strip, the first in a series, is produced by the computer from information on the flight plan. Each successive controller will use these to guide the aircraft through his area.

Airways are like huge motorways in the sky. They are corridors of airspace ten miles wide, usually from a base of between 5,000 and 7,000ft up to a height of 24,500ft. Above the airways are Upper Air Routes which cater for high flying aircraft. Every airway is given a code colour and a number, like Green 1 or White 39.

Separation Distances must be maintained between aircraft. In controlled airspace an aircraft may not pass within five nautical miles of another, if it is at the same height. If two aircraft are less than five nautical miles apart horizontally, they must be at least 1,000 ft apart vertically.

Radar is continuously tracking the position and height of each aircraft. A beam of energy is transmitted through an aerial and reflected back from the aircraft being tracked. Primary surveillance radar is used to give the aircraft's position over the ground. Secondary surveillance radar is used to give its identity, height and destination.

Identity of an aircraft consists of the flight number which becomes the radio call sign. All aircraft flying north or east have even numbers, while those flying south or west have odd numbers.

The Transponder is a device on the aircraft which automatically transmits its identity and destination when "questioned" by the radar. The aircraft's radio altimeter gives its height.

The Radar Screen, closely watched by the Air Traffic Controller, presents all this information superimposed on a map of the airways. Each aircraft blip is labelled with its identity, height and route.

A Stack is formed by aircraft waiting their turn to land at busy peak times. Aircraft approaching their destination airport are directed by the Air Traffic Control Centre (ATCC) to reporting points, located by radio beacons. When aircraft arrive more quickly than the airport can land them, they are instructed to circle at different heights over the beacon. As each aircraft is called in to the airport from the bottom of the stack, so those above move down 1,000ft.

Approach Control is responsible for aircraft from the moment when the ATCC hands them over, until they have been lined up to land on one of the runways.

Aerodrome Control takes over at this point. It operates from the Visual Control Room at the top of the ATC tower and controls aircraft on their final approach to land, when they are preparing for departure, when they are taxiing and during actual take off.

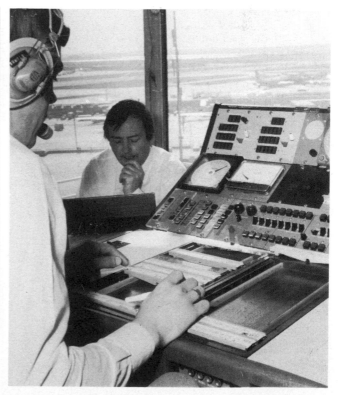

Above: *The Air Traffic Control Centre at West Drayton monitors progress of aircraft en route.* **Right:** *On final approach, taxiing and taking off, aircraft are controlled from the Visual Control Room of the tower at Heathrow.*

Things to do

1. WHAT HAVE YOU LEARNT?

Junior

a) *Remote mountain valleys were first made accessible by:*
   – cars ☐
   – telephone ☐
   – railways ☐

b) *The post bus:*
   – collects postmen to come to work ☐
   – carries people, goods and mail to remote communities ☐
   – is like a travelling grocer ☐

c) *The Alpine barrier has been overcome by building:*
   – flyovers ☐
   – underpasses ☐
   – road and rail tunnels ☐

d) *Rack and pinion is:*
   – a form of medieval torture ☐
   – a new form of shop display ☐
   – a type of railway built for steep climbs ☐

e) *A number of climatic hazards can delay aircraft:*
   – birds ☐
   – fog ☐
   – clouds ☐

Intermediate

a) *Every man, woman and child in Switzerland takes about how many cable car trips a year?*
   – 50 ☐
   – 100 ☐
   – 220 ☐

b) *The longest road tunnel in the world is the:*
   – St. Gotthard ☐
   – Mont Cenis ☐
   – Mont Blanc ☐

c) *The Matterhorn was first climbed in:*
   – 1859 ☐
   – 1865 ☐
   – 1888 ☐

d) *To prevent aeroplanes from skidding, icy runways are sprayed with:*
   – glucose ☐
   – anti-freeze ☐
   – glycol ☐

e) *A stack:*
   – is a tall factory chimney ☐
   – a hand of cards ☐
   – a holding pattern for aircraft waiting to land ☐

Advanced

a) *Modern forms of transport were introduced in the mountains:*
   – for political reasons ☐
   – as a shrewd investment ☐
   – to reduce isolation ☐

b) *The Alps were included on the Grand Tour because:*
   – of morbid curiosity ☐
   – of their scenic beauty ☐
   – the aristocrats wanted to go skiing ☐

c) *The Alpine mountain passes are open:*
   – all the year ☐
   – only for part of the year ☐
   – only if you go on foot with guides ☐

d) *The decision on whether to land a plane rests with:*
   – the captain of the aircraft ☐
   – air traffic control ☐
   – runway patrols ☐

e) *The purpose of major road building programmes in mountain regions is:*
   – to attract ever-increasing numbers of tourists ☐
   – to remove through traffic from congested settlements ☐
   – to concentrate traffic on a few principal routes ☑

2. FLYING TIME

In the departure lounge

Study the flight departures board, and using the information on it write down here:

a) The number of different airlines shown ....
b) The total number of departure gates..............................
c) How many different destinations are shown ....
d) Your own flight number ....
e) The time of departure of your flight...............................
f) The departure gate for your flight ....

In the aircraft

a) What make of aircraft are you flying in? ....
b) How many passengers can it hold? ....
c) How many hostesses and stewards are there?............
d) How many emergency exits are there? ....
e) Where are they located? ....
f) What two instructions must be obeyed by all passengers before take-off? ....
....
g) Which section of the air traffic control system will guide the pilot out on to the runway and direct take-off? ....
....
h) What is the cruising speed of your aircraft? ....

3. THE CHANGING VILLAGE

In winter mountains used to be cut off from the outside world for nearly half the year. People rarely went beyond their own valleys. As a result of this they were often out of touch with the rest of the world and not keen on changing their way of life. Over the last century trains, buses, cars and telephones have all helped to break down this isolation.

Imagine you are an old farmer who has spent all his life in a remote mountain village. Suddenly the development of the village into a ski resort brings crowds of tourists. Write a letter to a friend in another village describing how communications have changed and how this has changed your life.

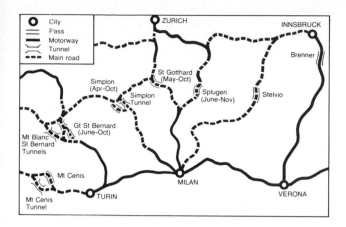

4. TRAFFIC FLOW

To ensure a rapid flow of traffic through the mountains there are many passes and tunnels through the Alps. The diagram shows the principal roads into Northern Italy over the Alps and the times of year when they are open.

a) You are driving a heavy lorry from Zurich to Verona in March. The weather is uncertain. The Simplon Tunnel is closed for repairs. Which would be the quickest, easiest and safest route for you to take?

b) What would be the effect on a modern ski resort, if it was cut off for two weeks, by a heavy snowfall.

5. ON THE WAY

On the journey to your resort, make a list of all the different forms of transport you used from the moment you left home until the moment you arrived at your hotel. How long did you spend in each form of transport, and how far did you travel in each form of transport? With this information draw a graph like the one shown and answer these questions.

a) Which part of the journey took the longest time and why? reaching the airport; the flight; travelling from the airport to your resort.

b) Which was the fastest form of transport?

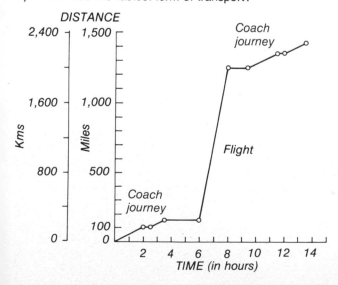

6. PROJECT – TRAFFIC CENSUS

You can carry out your own traffic census to find out about traffic movements in your resort. Split the class into groups and give each group a different point in the resort to collect information. At certain agreed times each person collects the same information. This will vary according to your resort, but should include:

the number of cars that pass by; the number of lorries; the number of buses; the number of bicycles; the registration plates of lorries, cars or buses; the number of pedestrians; can you tell where they came from?

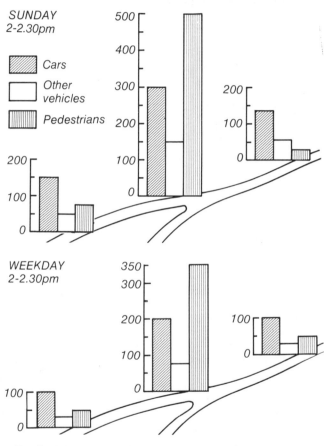

Put the information you collect on to a graph, like the ones above, showing the time of day and the numbers of cars, people or lorries. Using your graph and the information collected, decide:

a) Which are the busiest times of day for:
cars; lorries; coaches; pedestrians.

b) Which are the busiest times of the week for:
cars; lorries; coaches; local buses.

c) Which are the least busy times of the day or week for:
cars; lorries; coaches; local buses.

d) Which is the busiest part of the resort?

e) Can you suggest any reasons for the busy and less busy times?

f) Are the movements of people and traffic the same as you might find at home. For example, if Sunday is the quietest day of week at home, is it the same in your resort? If not, why not?

IX. Mountain myths and customs

For most ancient peoples mountain regions were places to be avoided. But they could hardly be ignored, for they were places of mystery, of thunder, lightning and volcanic eruptions. They were also closest to the sun, the moon and the stars – regarded as gods in much of the ancient world.

Gods and mountains

In Greek mythology Mount Olympus was the throne of Zeus and home of the gods. The volcano, Mount Etna, was a huge forge where Hephaestus, the blacksmith god, made thunderbolts for Zeus helped by the giant, one-eyed Cyclops.

In Japan Mount Fuji has always been considered as a holy mountain. In Africa tribes in the Congo believed that vertigo was caused by the souls of the dead who lived in the mountains. In the Christian world, too, mountains have a special significance. Moses was given the Ten Commandments on Mount Sinai. Even today, mountains are used as symbols. Four American presidents have been immortalised in giant sculptures on the face of Mount Rushmore, South Dakota, USA.

Pagan versus Christian

The folklore of Europe had its origins in Greek, Roman and Teutonic legends. Remarkably similar characters, like the trolls of Scandinavia, the ovio of Italy and the vila of Yugoslavia, appear in different places with different traditions.

On long winter evenings round warm fires people told stories of Ullr, the Scandinavian (and German) god of winter, hunting and archery, who had his home on top of the Alps, and dwarfs who mined precious metals under the mountains. With the coming of the Christian Church these tales were replaced or altered to accommodate the new Christian beliefs. Only in Scandinavia did the pagan tales continue to be told.

Despite the Church's influence many old customs and legends remained. They were similar to ancient traditions found throughout the world. In Switzerland, Norway, India, Australia and Rumania there are traditional sunset rituals which are very similar. Blowing a musical instrument – the alphorn in Switzer-land – is supposed to prolong daylight. A story of a warrior who saves himself from a dragon's pit by hanging on to the dragon's tail as it climbs out, is told in places as far apart as the Alps, Poland and China.

Festivals

The farmer's year, historical events and church celebrations are the basis of most traditional festivals.

The coming of spring, after a long winter spent mostly indoors, is an occasion to celebrate. In March there are spring festivals, like the Lucerne Carnival in Switzerland. Only 100 years ago in remote parts of the French Alps people would sit down to ceremonial meals of omelettes to celebrate the first egg collections.

These festivals were older than Christianity, but the Church incorporated them into its own calendar. Spring festivals tie in neatly with Easter. The Lucerne Carnival takes place just before Lent. Mid-winter festivals can be linked with Christmas.

Autumn festivals have remained purely agricultural, as there are no important Christian celebrations at that time of year. The various harvests were celebrated, as was the bringing down of the cows from the alps.

Costumes

The rich embroidery and lacework of Sunday-best costumes seen at today's festivals is rather different from the clothes normally worn by ordinary

Right: *The sacred mountain, Mount Fuji, rises majestically above the clouds.*

people in the mountains. They made their clothes from local materials. A man's leather trousers were made to last through many years of work in the fields. In the Austrian Tyrol people wore lederhosen, shorts or breeches made from chamois leather. Coats were made of wool with chamois horn buttons. Hats were adorned with eagle feathers.

It was not until the eighteenth century that what is now considered as traditional costume developed. As the mountain economy improved people could afford brighter clothing. The Catholic Church encouraged special Sunday dress. Better communications allowed traders to visit remote areas, offering new materials for the women to make into bright costumes.

Above left: *New Year demons at Appenzell, Switzerland. In February the man of straw costume is burnt to celebrate the end of winter.* **Above right:** *People in colourful costumes taking part in a festival at Ljubljana, Yugoslavia.*
Left: *Illustration by Arthur Rackham of Grimm's fairy tale about the valiant tailor, who challenged a giant to contests of crushing rocks and tossing boulders. Giants were believed to have made the rock-strewn mountain landscape.*

Mountains at war

Throughout history, mountains in many parts of the world have played key roles in many wars. They act as natural frontiers, which must be crossed by invading armies. They make perfect hideouts for irregular troops and partisans.

Italy's Alpine frontier

The Alps have not always been the ideal frontier for Italy that they are today. Almost up to the time of Christ, Gaul extended south as far as the Arno river, on which Florence stands. This part was known as Cisalpine Gaul, as opposed to Transalpine Gaul, north of the mountains. It was the southern Gauls who sacked Rome in 390BC. They did not have to cross the mountains to do so.

This leaves Hannibal and the Carthaginians the distinction of being the first to make a full scale military crossing of the Alps. They came through Spain, crossing the Pyrenees without too many difficulties. An army of 60,000 men and 37 elephants crossed the Rhône on rafts, before attempting the Alps. There their problems began. They were attacked by plundering Gauls. Men and animals fell sick. Food was short. Eventually they reached the top. Hannibal addressed his men: "Soldiers, you are

crossing not only the ramparts of Italy, but the very walls of Rome!" But still their troubles were not over. The descent was awful. Less than half the men who set out made the crossing. Hannibal himself lost an eye. Yet they marched on south, and never lost a battle on Roman soil.

By AD 180 the Romans had made crossing the Alps as easy as it was to be for 1,700 years. There were at least five paved roads, using the Great and Little Saint Bernard, Splügen, Maloja and Brenner passes.

These same roads were to make the barbarian invasions which destroyed Rome easier – not that the Huns and Vandals found the Alps an impassable barrier.

Napoleon was the next man to attempt an invasion through the Alps. His crossing was almost as difficult as Hannibal's. But it made him the master of Italy, by being able to defeat the Austrians at the battle of Marengo in 1800.

The last major war to be fought in the Alps was the Italian-Austrian front, during World War 1. There again, the mountains were almost as much of an enemy as the rival armies. As many as 40,000 men died in avalanches, snow and extreme conditions.

Guerrillas and mountains

Modern guerrilla warfare dates back to the Peninsula War (1808-14). Napoleon's army lost half a million men in Spain. They were harrassed by Portugese and Spanish guerrillas (Spanish for "little war"), supported by the British Navy and later by troops under the command of Sir John Moore and Arthur Wellesley, soon to be made the Duke of Wellington.

The Peninsular War demonstrated two aspects of modern guerrilla warfare that still hold true. Firstly, irregular soldiers are most effective if fighting for an ideology. The Spaniards were among the first to fight with the spirit of nationalism – quite a new concept at the beginning of the last century. Secondly, guerrilla warfare is the only hope of less sophisticated fighters against well equipped modern armies.

As the leading industrial and imperial nation of the nineteenth century, Britain was often the target of guerrilla warfare. The North-West frontier of India was the scene of periodic fighting throughout the time of the British Raj. Writers like Henty and Kipling encouraged highly romanticised views of this kind of warfare. Places like the Khyber Pass became household names.

It was in Afghanistan that the British were to encounter their fiercest opposition. The various Afghan wars ended with British recognition of Afghanistan's independence in 1919. Like the British, the Russians are now finding the rugged mountains and determined tribesmen a formidable combination.

In the Boer war, again British regular troops were pinned down by local forces, which knew the countryside. The British were even forced to abandon their traditional red uniforms in favour of camouflage khaki before they gained victory.

More recently there have been striking examples of victories by guerrillas operating from mountains. In the two years from October 1934 Mao Tse-Tung led 100,000 men in the famous Long March through some of the most mountainous country in China. With his army intact, he was able to take power in 1949. During the second world war Marshal Tito led one of the most successful resistence movements against the Germans, in the mountains of Yugoslavia.

Above: *Moving guns through the mountains of Afghanistan, where British forces from India met fierce opposition from guerrillas.*

Left: *Hannibal lost half his army of 60,000 men crossing the Alps in 218BC.* **Above:** *Marshal Tito at his mountain hideout during World War II. Tito led the Yugoslav partisans against the Germans.* **Below:** *Napoleon's army crossing the Great Saint Bernard Pass, May 1800.*

Surmounting the barriers

Today we have a romantic view of the mountains – glorious scenery, picturesque people and places. But that view is a mere two hundred years old. Throughout the rest of Europe's recent history the Alps have been nothing more than a barrier to progress.

The mountains were a physical barrier in that they were difficult to cross. They were also a barrier to the passage of ideas. They were inhabited by backward, superstitious people, who believed that dragons lived among the peaks and giants thundered in gorges and shrugged down landslides.

Spreading the Renaissance

As a result of the sacking of Rome by the Goths and other invaders, Western Europe was left without a cultural centre. For almost a thousand years of the Dark Ages people forgot the achievements of the ancient Greek and Roman civilisations.

In the late 1300s writers and artists in Italy rediscovered classical learning. But the effects of this rebirth (the meaning of the word Renaissance) did not reach Northern Europe, the other side of the Alps, for many years. In the case of Britain the full effects were not felt until nearly a century later.

From then on, the Europeans' attitude to everything, including their mountains, began to change. The first man who is recorded as actually enjoying climbing mountains is Konrad von Gesner, a doctor, who climbed Mount Pilatus in 1555, because he thought it would give him exercise and a pleasant experience.

Early scientific curiosities, like crystal hunting, took people to the Alps. Communications improved. The eighteenth century Age of Enlightenment and the new ideas that were to be the basis of the French Revolution completed a turnabout in attitudes towards the mountains. Suddenly they begin to feature in art, poetry, music and philosophy.

Art in the mountains

Philosopher Jean Jacques Rousseau was one of the first to appreciate the mountains. Artists like Turner painted in the Alps. Lake Geneva (Lac Léman in French), the largest of the Alpine lakes, was celebrated by Lord Byron, in the Childe Harold's Pilgrimage: "The mirror where the stars and mountain view, the stillness of their aspect in each trace . . ."

The Grand Tour became an essential part of every rich young Englishman's education. The Industrial Revolution had produced a class of well-off, well-educated but idle young gentlemen, who energetically improved themselves by making the Grand Tour of Europe.

In the early nineteenth century three of the greatest English poets, Byron, Shelley and Keats, were at one time or another living and working in Italy. Byron and Shelley also spent a considerable amount of time in Switzerland.

The romantic movement quickly took remote mountain areas to its heart. In the Lake District, Wordworth celebrated the hills. The mountains of Scotland featured in the novels of Sir Walter Scott. The mountains of Norway inspired the composer Grieg. His Peer Gynt Suite was based on a Norse legend.

Conquering the peaks

At the same time a new kind of mountain enthusiast appeared – the Alpinist, or climber. One of the most famous of all, Edward Whymper, was both artist and mountaineer. He earned his living making engravings and climbed as a hobby.

Mountaineering began with the first ascent of Mont Blanc, in August 1786. But dramatic developments were slow to come after that, during the years of the French Revolution and the Napoleonic wars. However, with the return of peace many climbers, mostly English, returned to the Alps, scaling the main peaks one after the other.

By the 1860s most had been climbed. Only the Matterhorn remained of the giants in the Alps. Edward Whymper tried unsuccessfully eight times in five years to reach the summit. He was determined to succeed ahead of his great rival, the Italian Jean-Antoine Carrel. Finally, having chosen a new route, he reached the top on July 14, 1865. Carrel and his party were only 350m (1,200ft) below, on another route. But Whymper's triumph was marred by an accident on the way down, in which four of his party were killed. Carrel reached the top three days later.

With the Matterhorn conquered, serious climbers began to attack other peaks throughout the world. Most of the highest mountains had been climbed before the beginning of the first world war. In 1953 Mount Everest was finally scaled by Tenzing Norkay and Edmund Hillary.

Today, new barriers of endurance and skill are being attempted. Rock climbers are ascending vertical walls, previously thought to be unclimbable. And in 1978 two Austrians, Messner and Habeler, reached the summit of Everest without the aid of oxygen.

Top: *Developments by Renaissance artists like Leonardo da Vinci were slow to cross the Alps.* **Above:** *Poets like Byron made the mountains popular.*

Peter Taugwalder Sohn
Nov. 1843-1923.

Edward Whymper
1840-1911.

Peter Taugwalder
Vater. 1820-1888.

Lord f. Douglas
1847-1865

Rev. Chs. Hudson
1828-1865

D. Hadow
1846-1865.

Michel A. Croz
1830-1865.

Die ersten Besteiger des
Matterhorns 14 Juli 1865
in der Reihenfolge des Abstieges, nach zeitgemässen Aufnahmen.
Oben die drei damals Ueberlebenden. Zusammengestellt v. P. Montandon

Above: *An avalanche in Switzerland by Turner. He and other artists recognised the beauty of the Alps.* **Left** *and* **below:** *Whymper was the first to climb the Matterhorn, but four of his party (bottom row) were killed.*

Things to do

1. MIX AND MATCH

Match the dates, figures or lengths of time with the events.

Junior

- The appearance of first skeleton fossils — 4,500 million years ago
- The Alps and Himalayas folded — 3,800 million years ago
- The oldest mountain areas formed — 600 million years ago
- The earth was formed — 200 million years ago
- All the continents still joined — 25 million years ago

Intermediate

- The thickness of the crust beneath the Alps — 150 million years' time
- The appearance of the first dinosaurs — 13m (43ft) every 1000 years
- The current rate of mountain building — 40,000km (25,000 miles)
- When Africa and Europe will overlap — 60km (37 miles)
- The length of the Mid-Atlantic ridge — 225 million years ago

Advanced

- Wegener propounded the theory of continental drift — 200 million years ago
- Thickness of earth's skin of sedimentary rocks — 1,000,000 years
- The poles were reversed — 2.5km (1.6 miles)
- The continents began to drift apart — 430 million years ago
- The time taken to join England and France at the present rate of continental drift — 60 years ago

---

2. MAKING THE MOST OF THE LAND

One of the problems facing mountain farmers is the small size and scattered positions of their land holdings. This may be due to tradition or to the fact that the farmer has inherited fields in different places around the village. **Consolidation** means reorganising the fields so that one farmer has all his fields together and can farm them without having to travel to the other side of the village. Look at this diagram of consolidation.

Junior

a) What do you notice about the land belonging to the farmer before consolidation? How many separate parcels of land did he own? How were they distributed? How far would the farmer travel if he wanted to visit each parcel in one day?

b) What happened to the parcels of land after consolidation? How many parcels of land does the farmer have now and how are they distributed? How far does he have to walk now to visit all his fields?

Intermediate

a) What are the problems the farmer faced before consolidation?

b) What advantages does consolidation bring the farmer?

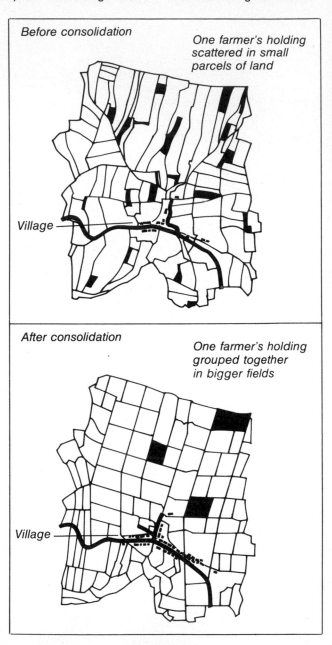

Before consolidation

One farmer's holding scattered in small parcels of land

Village

After consolidation

One farmer's holding grouped together in bigger fields

Village

Advanced

The photograph on page 46 shows that the parcels of land on the terraces are not only small, but also awkward to reach, especially when carrying farming tools.

a) How is farming carried out on such steep slopes?

b) Where did the materials used to build the terraces come from?

c) In the Alps terraces are often used nowadays to grow grapes. What might you find growing on terraces in other parts of the world?

3. WATERS OF THE EARTH

Junior
Find out the names of any mineral water bottled near your resort. Is it fizzy or still? If you can speak the language, look on the label to see if you can discover what this particular water is good for.

Intermediate
For centuries people have been going to spas to cure their health problems. Find out whether there are any spas near your resort. How long has there been a spa there? Is it still a spa today? Are there any spas in Britain?

A nineteenth century print of public baths in Switzerland.

Look at the picture above of a public spa baths in the last century. What are the people in the water doing to amuse themselves? Why would they have to find something to do while they were in the water? Would you be likely to see a similar scene in a modern spa? If not, what would a modern spa session look like?

Advanced
Many commercially bottled mineral waters are naturally filtered through many layers of geological strata.
a) Draw a diagram showing layers of permeable and impermeable rock in a structure that would provide filtered water for a mountain spring. Show where the water comes from.
b) What is the **water table**, and what effect does it have on the location of mountain springs?
c) Give three reasons why you might use bottled spring water, rather than tap water.

---

4. MOUNTAIN AND LOWLAND FARMS

Here are some results from a French government survey in the Rhone-Alps region.

	Mountainous areas	Lowland areas
Number of farms	48,052	68,355
Area of farmland	711,231h	1,015,090h
Area suitable for cereal crops	67,758h (9%)	316,653h (31%)
Area suitable for grazing	521,616h (73%)	384,411h (38%)

a) Why are mountainous areas less suitable for cereal crops than lowland areas?
b) Why is more land suitable for grazing in mountain areas than in lowland areas?

5. PROJECT – RECORDING TEMPERATURES AND RAINFALL

From reference books or while at your resort, collect the local temperature and rainfall statistics and make up histograms similar to those in the diagram above.
a) How many months have temperatures below freezing point (°C)?
b) What was the first date on which snow fell:
  – over the last 10 years?
  – over the last 20 years?
c) In the same period what was the date when the snow disappeared?
d) At what height is the snow line at or near your resort?

---

6. PROJECT – WHOSE FAULT?

On page six you have read it has taken thousands of millions of years to build the earth. Its various structural formations have been evolving throughout that time. But occasionally, dramatic events, such as earthquakes, can concertina thousands of years of evolution into a few seconds.

Here is an experiment which reproduces the processes which cause faulting and folding, two of the commonest structural formations in rocks.

Take a wooden box and replace one side with a sheet of glass so you will be able to see the experiment taking place. Put a wooden divider across the middle of the box and hold it in place while you fill the box with layers of sand, ashes and soft clay to simulate the layers of sedimentary rock. Push the divider slowly to one side and see what happens.

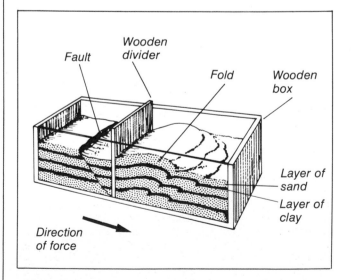

a) What happens to the horizontal layers of "rock" when a force is exerted?
b) Does it make any difference from which side the force is exerted?
c) What happens if the force is maintained over a long period?
d) What happens if the force is stopped?

X. France

France is the second largest country in Europe and over twice the size of the United Kingdom. Within its frontiers it has an amazing variety of landscapes, including five major mountain areas – the Alps, the Pyrenees, the Jura, the Massif Central and the Vosges.

The Massif Central is in the centre of the country, in a province called the Auvergne. Both this and the Vosges, which border the river Rhine, along the German frontier, are regions of old, hard rocks, dating from the Cambrian period, some 600 million years ago. The newer, higher mountain ranges run along two other important frontiers. In the south the Pyrenees separate France from Spain, and in the south east the Alps separate France from Italy and Switzerland.

As well as a variety of landscapes, France has many different climatic zones. In the north and north west, conditions are typically temperate, similar to the climate of England. Towards the east and south it becomes gradually warmer and drier. The east has much colder winters than the west, where the sea introduces milder air. In the south the climate is Mediterranean with hot, dry summers and mild, wet winters. It is not surprising that most tourists in France head south!

Within the major climatic divisions there are a number of local variations, known as micro-climates. Among the best known is the Mistral, a wind which is funneled from north to south down the valley of the river Rhône.

Tropical crops

Because of the variety of climates, the crops grown in France range from potatoes and oats, typical of colder northern climates, to sub-tropical plants, like tobacco. There are even some tropical crops, like rice, which is grown in the marshy Carmargue, on the delta of the river Rhône.

France's wines are famous throughout the world. Champagne, Burgundy and Beaujolais are just a few of the best known, named after the regions, in which they are produced.

Moving to the city

With the increasing rationalisation and mechanisation of agriculture, fewer people are needed to work on the land. Many have been attracted to better paid factory jobs in the cities. Yet France, with a slightly smaller population than Britain, still has more people working on the land than the UK. And French farmers are a powerful force in French politics.

In parts of regions like the Massif Central, however, rural depopulation has gone so far that whole villages have been deserted. Meanwhile 16 per cent of the French population now live in the Paris area, the largest industrial centre as well as the capital.

To accommodate such large movements of people, new towns have been built round Paris and other major cities like Lyons. Some provincial centres, such as Toulouse and Strasbourg, have been designated *metropoles d'equilibre,* or growth poles, to which industry is encouraged to migrate. The next level of settlements, including market towns like Cahors, Limoges and Tours, are known as *moyennes villes.* They are being given facelifts to encourage smaller businesses to move there and provide local employment.

France's changing face

The traditional picture of France – of a country in which all shops and offices close for two hours at midday, while everyone enjoys a magnificent lunch – is changing fast. Paris is a busy metropolis all day, and it seems, all night.

In May 1981 there was another sharp break with tradition. After 23 years of government by the parties of the centre-right, elections brought to power first a Socialist President, Francois Mitterand, and then a Socialist Parliamentary majority. The government is committed to far-reaching changes, like the nationalisation of banks and major industries.

Savoy and Piedmont

Being geographically separate from most of the rest of France, it is not surprising that the French Alps have more historical links with Italy than with Paris. Since Roman times the area has been strategically important because of the mountain passes. For over a thousand years these were controlled by the independent Dukes of Savoy. Their capital was the city of Chambéry.

Gradually the power of the central government in Paris grew at the expense of the power of the Dukes. In 1860 Savoy became part of France. But this was not the end of the ruling family. The Dukes became Kings of

Mont Blanc, the highest mountain in Europe (4,807m, 15,771ft), was first climbed in August 1786. The climbers were a local doctor, Michel-Gabriel Paccard and a guide, Jacques Balmat. Dr Paccard's aims were scientific, but Balmat's interest was financial — in 1760 a Swiss professor had offered a reward to the first person to climb Mont Blanc. The two men climbed for two days, reaching the summit in the dark — all without ropes.

Things to do

1. Match the shops with the things you would be able to buy in each of them.

Une baguette   L'épicerie
Du fromage   La boulangerie
Du jambon   La confiserie
Des bonbons   La charcuterie

2. On bottles of what would you expect to find the following words printed?
V.S.O.P.
Appellation controlée
Déclaré d'intérêt public
V.D.Q.S.

3. Why is the train from Paris to the south coast called the Mistral? Can you find out if there are any other trains in France with names?

4. Here is a list of the four largest cities in France. Match each with its population figures.

Paris   1.2 million
Lille   1.0 million
Lyons   0.9 million
Marseilles   8.5 million

5. Draw a map of France to show the following:
   a) How the mountains form natural frontiers for France
   b) The major climatic zones of France
   c) Three major wine growing regions
   d) France's four largest cities.

The Tour de France is the toughest cycle race in the world, with 130 competitors covering 4,000km (2,500 miles) in 20 days. Every year the route for the race changes, but it always includes stages through the Alps and the Pyrenees, with the final stage ending in Paris. The difficult mountain stages demand great determination from the riders. In one 17km (10.5 miles) hillclimb up the Col de la Madeleine in the Alps riders climb from 471m (1,545ft) to 1,993m (6,539ft) in just over an hour.

Above is Joop Zoetemelk, 1980 winner, wearing the leader's yellow jersey, on an Alpine stage.

Sardinia and Piedmont, in northern Italy, with their capital at Turin. And in 1871 Victor Emmanuel II of Piedmont became the first King of all Italy.

Food from France

French food is known as the best in the world. Every region has its own specialities. Like many mountain areas, Savoy is famous for its dairy products. Many dishes are prepared *au gratin* (with cheese) and in France a cheese fondue is known as a *fondue Savoyarde*. Other special cheese from the French Alps are Reblochon and Tomme de Savoie, creamy cheeses made from cow's milk.

Some of the best souvenirs to bring back from France are food specialities. The long crusty loaves come in several sizes from *un pain* (the largest) through *une baguette* and *une flute* to *une ficelle* (the smallest). Cheeses make marvellous presents – as long as they are well wrapped in your bag!

The département jigsaw

The whole of France is divided into départements, which are like British counties. The départements are listed in alphabetical order and each has a number, which is also used in postal codes and on car number plates. For example the cars from central Paris have numbers ending with 75. Those from the Paris suburbs end in 73, 77, 78, 92, or 95. The mountain départements of Hautes Alpes and Haute Savoie have the numbers 05 and 74 respectively.

Money matters

The currency of France is the French **franc.** Some of the most famous Frenchmen are portrayed on the notes.

The notes exist in denominations of 10, 50, 100, 500 and 1,000 francs. The 10 franc notes are becoming rarer as they are being replaced by coins. Other coins are the one, two and five franc pieces. Two franc coins are a recent introduction. There are 100 **centimes** to a franc in coins of five, 10, 20 and 50 centimes.

Switzerland

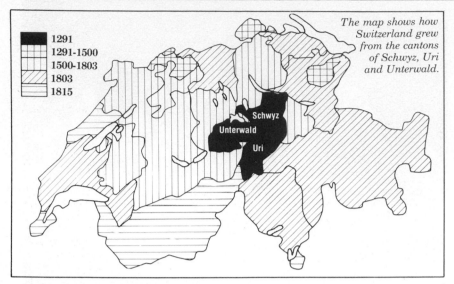

1291
1291-1500
1500-1803
1803
1815

The map shows how Switzerland grew from the cantons of Schwyz, Uri and Unterwald.

Schwyz
Unterwald
Uri

Switzerland breaks all the rules of nationhood. It is made up of 27 independent cantons, with four official languages and two different religions. Yet, despite such diversity, it has one of the longest traditions of independent self-rule in Europe.

The map shows how Switzerland has grown from its modest beginnings in 1291, when representatives from the three cantons of Schwyz, Uri and Unterwalden met near Lake Lucerne to plan how to free themselves from their Austrian rulers.

After fierce fighting they won their independence in 1315. Gradually other cantons joined the Confederation and, united, the Swiss defended their freedom against all comers until the French defeated them in 1515.

Only in 1648 under the Treaty of Westphalia was Switzerland again recognised as a sovereign state. One hundred and fifty years later it became a republic. Since then the Swiss have tried to remain strictly neutral.

Europe's United States
In some ways Switzerland was a forerunner of America's United States. Each canton, like an American state, has a large measure of control over what happens within its boundaries.

Important national decisions are often voted on in a referendum, rather than decided in Parliament. A referendum can be called when the signatures of 100,000 citizens have been collected.

Yet until 1971 Switzerland could hardly be called a democracy, since only the men were allowed to vote! The woman's traditional role was summed up by the Swiss saying: Kirche, Küche, Kinder (church, cooking, children).

Beneath the calm surface of the cantons there lie some tensions. These recently resulted in the formation of the twenty seventh canton, called Jura. Despite its name, it does not include the whole of the mountainous Jura region, but only the northern French-speaking half. In the referendum called to decide the matter, the southern German-speaking population voted overwhelmingly to remain as part of the canton of Berne – also German-speaking.

Do you speak Swiss?
Nearly three quarters of Switzerland is German-speaking. About 20 per cent of the people speak French as their first language and four per cent Italian. The remaining one per cent (about 50,000 people) speak Romansch, which originates from Latin and survives in the Grisons area of central Switzerland. Romansch has five major dialects. Often, people who speaking one dialect cannot understand others from a neighbouring valley.

Among the six and a half million people who live in Switzerland there are about 800,000 whose native language is more likely to be Greek, Turkish or even Serbo-Croat. They are the Gastarbeiter (literally guest workers) recruited to work in factories, on building sites and in hotels.

Town and country
Switzerland is land-locked. The coun-

try's only access to the sea is north, up the river Rhine through Germany.

The country is divided into three main geographical areas. The Alps, the highest part of the country, run approximately east to west, parallel with the Swiss-Italian frontier. The central plateau, running from Lake Geneva in the west to the Liechtenstein border in the east, is the richest agricultural region. In the north, the Jura mountains run north-east to south-west, parallel with the Swiss-French border.

The cities are situated on the central plateau. Berne is the capital, the centre of federal government, but it is less well known than cities like Geneva and Zurich.

Geneva is a sort of capital itself. Not only is it the European centre for the United Nations, but it is also the headquarters of many international organisations.

In the largest Swiss city, the 'Gnomes' of Zurich, as the financiers and bankers are nicknamed, handle huge sums of money deposited by investors from all over the world. The stability of Switzerland means that many companies and individuals deposit their funds in Swiss bank accounts. It is possible to have an account known only by a number.

Made in Switzerland
The height and climate of Switzerland make agriculture difficult. The best crop is grass, which can be grown even in the mountains. The result is that Switzerland's chief agricultural product is milk and other products which can be made from it, such as cheese or chocolate.

Nestlé, Tobler, Lindt and Suchard are the names of just four of the main chocolate producing firms. The first Swiss chocolate factory was opened in 1815 by Philippe Suchard. His successors today have no problems in selling chocolate at home for the Swiss eat more chocolate per head than anyone else in the world – 9.2 kg (20. 2 lbs) per person per year. The British come third behind the Belgians, consuming 6.6 kg (14.5 lbs) per person per year. Chocolate is certainly a serious business in Switzerland. The secrets of Lindt chocolate are even kept in a bank vault.

Until the last century Switzerland's principal exports were men to serve in mercenary armies, like the Vatican Guards. But today more than half the

Things to do

1. Try and collect examples of leaflets or product lables printed in two or three languages.
2. Describe the scene before, during and after William Tell's attempt to shoot the arrow off his son's head.
3. Imagine that you are the head of an international famine relief organisation, the head of a multi-national company or a multi-millionaire in your own right. What would be the advantages of having your headquarters and banking facilities in Switzerland?
4. Here is a list of world famous Swiss companies. Try to find out what each manufactures.
   Nestlé, Knorr, Rolex, Omega, Ciba-Geigy, Hoffman-La Roche, Brown Boveri, Oerlikon.
5. Try and find out about Switzerland's policy of neutrality, the system of national service and the civil defence programme. How does the Swiss view of national defence differ from the British?

Speaking the language

French is spoken by many Swiss people as well as the French. Here are a few phrases, which may help you speak to the people around you.

Good morning/day – *Bonjour*
Hi (informal) – *Salut*
Goodbye – *Au revoir*
Please – *S'il vous plaît*
Thank you – *Merci*
How are you? – *Ça va?*
Fine – *Ça va bien*
Sorry – *Pardon*
Excuse me – *Excusez-moi*
Where is? – *Où est?*
The toilet – *La toilette*
The doctor – *Le médecin*
The chemist – *La pharmacie*
Do you speak English? – *Parlez-vous anglais?*
Yes – *Oui*
No – *Non*
Do you have? – *Avez-vous?*
How much is it? – *C'est combien?*

Spot the Swiss

Car number plates in Switzerland consist of a two letter code, indicating the region in which the car is registered, followed by a sequence of numbers. Here are some examples to look out for: ZH is Zurich; LU is Lucerne; GE is Geneva; BE is Berne; VA is Valais. In Switzerland the number plate belongs to the car owner, rather than the car, so the plate is changed when the car is sold. There is a public register of number plates, so anyone can look up the name and address of the owner.

Shopping

The most typically Swiss souvenirs are cuckoo clocks (which used to be made by farmers in the winter, to pass the long days indoors and to make a little extra money), musical boxes, cow bells and Alphorns in miniature!), wood carvings, fine cotton fabrics, lace and chocolates.

On the menu

The most famous Swiss dish is the cheese fondue, for which there is a recipe on page 63. Raclette is a delicious mixture of partly melted cheese and potatoes served with gherkins. The national record for eating raclettes at one sitting stands at 24! From the German-speaking part of Switzerland comes Rösti, a fried potato cake. This is usually served with veal or pork.

people work in manufacturing industry, which tends to be specialised, sophisticated and highly international in outlook. Nestlé began as a local manufacturer of condensed milk, just over a 100 years ago. Today it has 300 factories all over the world and over 95 per cent of its business is conducted outside Switzerland.

One of the country's largest industries is tourism, both summer and winter. Since the establishment of the first ski schools in the 1930s, Switzerland has been able to offer some of the best winter sports facilities in the world – like those at the fashionable resorts of Davos, Gstaad, St Moritz and Klosters.

Money matters

Both France and Switzerland call their currency **francs**, but the values of each are very different.

The most common Swiss notes are worth 10, 20, 50 and 100 francs. There are also 500 and 1,000 franc notes, but they are rather valuable! At the other end of the scale you are likely to use 1, 2 and 5 franc coins. Each franc is divided into 100 **centimes** and the centime coins are worth 5, 10, 20 and 50c respectively.

At the end of the thirteenth century Switzerland was under the rule of the Austrian Empire. In the village of Altdorf the Austrian Governor, Gessler, put his hat at the top of a pole in the market place. He demanded that the people should bow to it as they passed. William Tell refused and was arrested. His punishment was to shoot an apple off his son's head with a crossbow. Tell took two arrows — the first to shoot the apple, the second to shoot the Governor, if anything happened to his son. He only needed one arrow, as his shot was accurate. Today the crossbow has been adapted as the hallmark of quality for Swiss produced goods.

A painting of William Tell by a famous Swiss artist, Ferdinand Hodler.

The Swiss Confederation was signed on the edge of Lake Lucerne in 1291.

Bulgaria

The first recorded inhabitants of the region we know as Bulgaria were the Thracians, who settled there in about 2,000BC. The Greek poet, Homer, wrote about them as a warlike and powerful people, yet they were also artists and craftsmen. They copied the best of classical Greek art from the Greek colonists, settling along the Black Sea coast.

In the fourth century BC Philip II of Macedon, ruler of Greece, conquered Thrace and founded a city called Philipopolis. Today it is called Plovdiv and its museum houses a magnificent collection of gold and silver works of Thracian art.

For a while the Romans controlled Thrace. But with the fall of Rome, Thrace was absorbed into the eastern part of the Roman Empire with its capital at Byzantium (later known as Constantinople). Barbarians invaded from the east and two tribes from the steppes of Russia, the Slavs and the Bulgars, merged to form the kingdom of Bulgaria – a satellite of Byzantium.

In spite of brief periods of independence, the country has been dominated from the east ever since. Turkey ruled Bulgaria for 500 years. The Russians invaded in 1944 (Bulgaria was allied with Germany) and the present Soviet-styled People's Republic was established in 1946. The country has been closely linked with Russia since then.

Bulgaria's four regions

Bulgaria is a rectangular country with four distinctive regions. In the north, the low, undulating Danube plain follows the river and also forms the frontier with Rumania. South of the Danube, and parallel to it, are the Balkan mountains. In the extreme south of the country lie the rugged Rhodope mountains. In between the two ranges is the Maritsa river.

Until the end of the Second World War Bulgaria was an almost entirely agricultural country. Since then there has been substantial industrialisation and several hydro-electricity schemes have been built in the mountains. Despite the drive to develop industry, Bulgaria is still a major agricultural producer, exporting wines, cereals, fruit and vegetables. Bulgaria is the home of yoghurt and also of a famous perfume, Attar of Roses.

In 1981 Bulgaria celebrates 1,300 years as a nation, making it one of the oldest in Europe. After a successful uprising against the Emperor of Byzantium in 681, a treaty was signed which recognised Bulgaria as a state for the first time. The soldiers below are wearing traditional uniforms from another important moment in Bulgarian history — liberation from 500 years of Turkish rule in 1879.

Money matters

The Bulgarian currency is called the **lev** (plural: leva). There are 100 **stotinki** to the lev. The notes you will come across are one, two, five, 10 and 20 leva. The coins are one, two and five leva, one, two, five, 10, 20 and 50 stotinki. You are not allowed to purchase Bulgarian currency outside the country, take it into the country or take it out at the end of your stay.

Private transport

Cars in Bulgaria may look familiar. Most of them are Russian Ladas, which can be seen in Britain. There is a Lada assembly plant at Bridlington. Letters on car number plates in Bulgaria indicate the town in which the car is registered, but as they are in Cyrillic script, they are difficult to decipher.

Shopping

Hand painted pottery (everything from individual pieces, to entire tea sets); hand woven table cloths and mats; wood carvings, painted wooden plates; leatherwork; copper Turkish coffee sets (more expensive).

Bulgarian cooking

Bulgarian food is plain, with few spices and seasonings, and many vegetables. Roast lamb, moussaka, kebabs and roast suckling pig are all considered delicacies. The original Bulgarian yoghurt was made from goat's milk, but it is now made from sheep's milk as well. Mixed with mineral water it becomes a drink known as airyan. It is also served as a cold soup, with chopped cucumbers, nuts, garlic and parsley, called tarator.

Speaking the language

This is difficult in Bulgaria! The Cyrillic alphabet is used all over Bulgaria. But in major towns, signs are apt to be written in four alphabets – Cyrillic, Turkish, Greek and Roman. All Bulgarians speak Bulgarian. Russian is their second language, German their third and English their fourth. So, it may help to know a few words in Bulgarian. But watch out for apparent contradictions. *Da* means yes, but it is accompanied by a sideways shake of the head. *Ne* is no, accompanied by a nod! *Molya* is please and *Merci* (as in French) is understood for thank you.

Yugoslavia

Modern Yugoslavia is essentially the creation of one man – Marshal Tito. Before his death in 1980 he had managed to forge a country out of a federation of six republics and five nationalities with four main languages, three religions and two alphabets.

In the north of the country there are rugged mountains, part of the Alpine chain, including the highest mountain in the country, Triglav, 2,863m (9,383ft). The Kars mountains of northern Yugoslavia have given their name to the karst land forms typical of limestone regions, with gorges, caves and castellated peaks. The Postojna caves with their giant stalactites and stalagmites, are the largest in Europe. They stretch 19km (12 miles) underground. Traces of ancient cave dwellers have been found there.

In the east the land flattens out towards the Danube, on which stands the federal capital, Belgrade. In the west the Adriatic coast is over 3,200km (2,000 miles) long. This beautiful shoreline, with more than 1,000 islands, draws crowds of tourists every year.

A checkered past

Like Bulgaria, the area which forms present-day Yugoslavia was conquered first by the Byzantines and later by the Turks. Parts of Yugoslavia were dominated by the Austrian Empire right up until 1918. Only then, with the establishment of the Kingdom of the Serbs, Croats and Slovenes, was full independence gained. The kingdom was renamed Yugoslavia in 1929, but the country remained united in name only.

In 1941 the bitter rivalries of the different national groups meant that the Germans were able to take control of the country in only two weeks.

From then on the Yugoslavs set about liberating themselves. Twenty per cent of the population died in the war. There were two main guerrilla armies, the Cetniks and the Communists under Tito. At first the Allies supported the Cetniks, but Tito's Partisans were obviously the stronger. They were also united under the banner of communism, rather than divided along national lines like the others.

This independent spirit has stayed with the Yugoslavs ever since. They have a unique brand of communism, under which factories, hotels and even banks belong to the workers.

Winter Olympics

In 1984 Sarajevo and its surrounding winter sports centres hosted the Winter Olympics, making Yugoslavia the first Eastern European country to stage the Winter Games. The resort of Jahorina, once a wartime partisan stronghold, staged the women's Alpine events, while the men's Alpine events were held in Bjelasnica. The bob-sleigh and toboggan runs were close to the centre of the city itself on Mount Trebevic.

The street corner in Sarajevo, Yugoslavia, where the Austrian Crown Prince Ferdinand was assassinated on June 28, 1914. This event brought about the beginning of World War 1.

Shopping

In craft shops there are many typical Yugoslavian items for sale. Look out for Norodna Radinost, traditional wood carvings. There are also beautiful examples of hand embroidery from all parts of the country, including the mountain regions of the north.

Yugoslavian food

The recipes and menus of Yugoslavia reflect the varied culture and history of the country. Dishes familiar to people from Western Europe appear alongside eastern specialities, like cevapcici (spiced minced meat, grilled), raznjici (pieces of pork or veal grilled on a spit), sarma (minced meat with rice and sauerkraut or vine leaves), moussaka (aubergines baked with minced meat) and Bosanski lonac (meaning Bosnian stew, which is a mixture of vegetables and meat). To round off the meal, Yugoslavs drink Turkish coffee (strong and sweet).

Money matters

The money used in Yugoslavia is the **dinar**, which is divided into 100 **para**. Notes worth 5, 10, 50, 100, 200, 500 and 1,000 dinar are in circulation, together with coins worth 5, 10, 20 and 50 para.

Currency regulations are somewhat easier in Yugoslavia than in many Eastern European countries. Yugoslavian currency in notes, up to a value of 1,500 dinar per person, can be brought into the country, provided that it is in notes of 100 dinar or less. No more than 1,000 dinar per person may be taken out of Yugoslavia at the end of the visit.

You may like to calculate in your workbook the present value of 1,500 and 1,000 dinar in pounds. You could also find out about postage rates, inside Yugoslavia and to Britain, with the equivalent value in pence.

Things to do

1. In 865AD the Bulgars were converted to Christianity and two monks, Cyril and Methodius, invented the Cyrillic alphabet, so that people could read the Christian texts.
   a) Look up in a guide book or an encyclopaedia the symbols of the Cyrillic alphabet. Write them down with their equivalents in our letters.
   b) Try to work out your name in Cyrillic letters.
2. The highest mountain in Bulgaria is called Musala. The highest mountain in Yugoslavia is called Triglav. From your atlas find out the height of both mountains in feet and metres.
3. Spartacus was a Thracian slave. Try to find out why he became famous in Rome in 73BC.
4. All these places are in, or associated with either Bulgaria or Yugoslavia, or both. Put Y or B, or both, next to each. Adriatic Sea ... Black Sea ... River Danube ... The Balkans ... Zagreb ... Sofia ... Rhodope Mountains ... Kars Mountains ...
5. Yugoslavia contains six republics, five nationalities, four main languages, three religions, and two alphabets. Try to find out the names of all of them.

Italy

Italy is dominated by two major mountain chains – the Alps and the Apennines. It is also the only area of Western Europe with active volcanoes. For Italy is in the centre of the mountain building activity which produced the Alps, and which is still pushing them up faster than erosion can wear them away.

The plate boundary between Africa and Europe runs across the Mediterranean, from Gibraltar to the north coast of Italy and then south east down the Italian coast. The active volcanoes of Vesuvius, Stromboli and Etna are all on faults near the plate margin. And the plate margin is also where earthquakes are most likely to occur, as happened with· the devastating 1980 earthquake in Central Italy.

The Apennines are a continuation of the Alps, running down the entire length of Italy, even into Sicily.

The other two dominant geographical features of Italy are the Alps and the valley of the River Po. The northern border of Italy runs along the top of the cluster of folded strata that make up the Alps. Erosion has carried away the upper layers in many places, but they are still visible in the lower mountains to the east – the Dolomites.

The spectacular, castellated (like a castle) formations of the Dolomites are the result of the way in which the sedimentary limestone, of which they are made, was laid down under the sea. It has thick horizontal layers (called beds) and vertical cracks (called joints). The individual blocks are eroded at different speeds, providing the jagged effect that has made the Dolomites famous.

The River Po drains the whole southern slope of the Italian Alps. During the Ice Age glaciers flowing north to south cut through the east-west folds of the mountains. Moraines blocked the valleys when the ice retreated, leaving lakes like Garda, Como amd Maggiore. The River Po, carrying an enormous amount of water and sediment from the mountains, has created a wide, flat plain right across the country. Trapped between the mountains, the Po valley has a slightly continental climate, with hot summers and cold winters.

Uniting Italy

Historically, the nation of Italy is a recent invention. Since the end of the Roman Empire, in the fifth century, the Italian peninsula had been divided into many small states. Napoleon conquered all of Italy and briefly united it. But after Napoleon's defeat at the Battle of Waterloo in 1815, Austria again took control of large parts of the north; Rome was given back to the Pope; Naples and Sicily were restored to their Spanish Bourbon king. Only the Kingdom of Sardinia and Piedmont, with its capital in Turin, remained independent.

After abortive revolutions in 1830 and 1848, the Piedmontese succeeded in taking Milan and Lombardy from the Austrians in 1859. A year later the nationalist revolutionary, Garibaldi, conquered the Kingdom of Naples and Sicily with his 1,000 red-shirted followers. Piedmont annexed all the central states, except Rome, in spite of being deserted by its French allies. King Victor Emmanuel of Piedmont was proclaimed King of Italy in 1861. Venice and the east remained part of the Austrian Empire until 1866. Rome finally became the capital of Italy in 1871.

North and south

The north of Italy is a thriving industrial area, while traditionally the south of Italy is agricultural and poor. Over the years many people from the south have moved north in search of jobs in factories, like the car and steel giant, Fiat, in Turin, which employes over 150,000 people.

The situation has become so serious that the Italian government has set up a special fund to encourage people to stay in the south. The fund is called the Cassa di Mezzogiorno. Mezzogiorno is the Italian name for the south of the country. The Common Market's Regional Development Fund also provides money to help set up factories there.

Taranto is one example of a town that has been chosen as a development area. Malarial marshes have been drained and agriculture improved through extensive irrigation schemes and the rationalisation of land holdings. Tourism has been promoted by the construction of hotels. To improve access to all these sites, roads and motorways have been vastly improved and extended.

Yet despite these efforts the south is falling even further behind the north. The north certainly has an advantage in its position. It is nearer to the main markets of north-west Europe. Lower transport costs make its products more competitive than those from the south.

Spectacular scenery is not normally a good enough reason for locating an industry in the mountains. Yet it was the reason that two brothers, Julius and Gilbert Durst, set up a postcard business in Brixen, in the Dolomites in the 1920s. To their surprise they soon found that the machine they had made to print the postcards was an even better proposition than the photographs of the mountains. Today Brixen is the headquarters of a multi-national company making photographic printing equipment, which is sold all over the world.

Money matters

Italian money can seem confusing because such large numbers are required to make even small purchases. A packet of chewing gum might cost you 200 lire. The currency is called the **lira** (plural: lire). There are notes worth 500, 1,000, 2,000, 5,000, 10,000, 20,000, 50,000 and 100,000 lire. Coins come in units of 5, 10, 20, 50, 100 and 200 lire.

Italian drivers

Sometimes it seems that the excitable Italian temperament is reflected in the way Italians drive. You may even be able to spot regional differences in driving habits by studying car number plates! Cars are registered by the town or province in which the owner lives. MI for Milan; TO for Turin; RO for Rome; BO for Bologna; SO for Sondrio (a mountain province in the Alps).

Regional dishes

One dish you may eat a lot of in Italy is pasta, made from flour, water and eggs. There are hundreds of different types – macaroni, vermicelli, capelli d'angeli (angel's hair). To cover the pasta there are dozens of different sauces. One of the best known is spaghetti Bolognese, with a sauce of minced meat and tomatoes.

Speaking the language

Italian is very simple to pronounce. Try out some of these phrases during your stay.

Good morning/good day –*Buon giorno*
Hi (very informal) –*Ciao (pron., chow)*
Goodbye –*Arrivederci*
Please –*Per favore*
Thank you –*Grazie*
How are you? – *Come sta?*
Fine (thank you) –*Bene (grazie)*
Sorry –*Mi scusi*
Don't mention it –*Prego*
Excuse me –*Permesso*
Where is? – *Dov'e?*
Do you speak English? –*Parla inglese?*
Yes –*Si*
No –*No*
Do you have? –*Ce l'ha?*
How much is it? –*Quanto costa?*
I should like –*Vorrei*
The bill –*Il conto*
Closed (shops) –*Chiuso*
Open –*Aperto*
Ladies (toilets) –*Signore (Donne)*
Gentlemen (toilets) –*Signori (Uomini)*

Italy has three active volcanoes: Etna in Sicily, the island of Stromboli, and the most famous of all, Vesuvius, near Naples. The photograph above shows the cloud of gas which rose from the crater in the last eruption in March 1944. The first recorded eruption of Vesuvius was in August AD 79, when over 2,000 people died as the Roman city of Pompeii was destroyed. Nearby Herculaneum was buried in 18m (60ft) of mud. Scientists think that another eruption of Vesuvius is quite likely, so an observatory has been set up to monitor volcanic activity in the mountain.

Things to do

1. Find out what the exchange rate is between the British pound and the Italian lira.
   a) How many pounds would you have if you were a lire millionaire?
   b) How many lire would you have if you were a pounds millionaire?
2. It is possible to go skiing in almost every part of Italy. Can you explain where and why you would be able to ski in the following places.
   a) Sicily
   b) Near Rome
   c) Sardinia
3. Using the map on page eight as a reference, draw a map of Italy showing:
   a) The boundaries of the African and Eurasian plates
   b) Italy's three active volcanoes
   c) The River Po and the Po plain
   d) The Apennines
   e) The area affected by the 1980 earthquake
4. The Vatican and San Marino are both in Italy geographically, but politically they are independent.
   a) Find out the reasons why they are separate states and who rules them.
   b) Locate both on your map of Italy.
   c) Name two other small independent states in Europe.

Austria

Austria today is not among the most powerful nations of the world, yet for nearly 700 years its ruling family, the Hapsburgs, dominated much of Europe. Their dominions included at various times Poland, Rumania, Hungary, Yugoslavia, Switzerland, parts of Italy, even the Netherlands and Spain. The end of the Austrian Empire came in 1918 with its defeat in the First World War. Emperor Charles I abdicated and Austria became a republic.

Because of its central position in Europe, Austria has always been a link between east and west. Before the birth of Christ, migrating tribes came up the Danube into Germany. The Turks twice besieged Vienna.

At the end of World War II the Russians, the British, the French and the Americans all occupied Austria. The country was divided into four zones, much as Berlin is today. It was only in 1955 that Austria regained its independence.

Mountains and plains

At its western end Austria narrows to only 48km (30 miles) wide. This is a mountainous region known as the Tyrol which is part of the Alps. The highest mountain in Austria – the Gross Glockner at 3,797m (12,457ft) – is in the Tyrol.

East of the Tyrol, between Salzburg and the Yugoslav border, is a lower mountainous region called the Chalk Alps. Here the mountains rise only to about 2,400m (8,000ft) and are thickly forested.

One of the main attractions in Vienna is the Spanish Riding School founded in 1572. The School gives riding displays in the Hofburg Palace (right). The horses used at the School are called Lipizzaners and are specially bred on a stud farm in the mountains. Originally the horses came from a stud farm in Lipizza in Italy and for this reason became known as Lipizzaners. At birth the foals are dark in colour, but their coats gradually lighten to grey or white. In the summer the young horses are taken up into the mountains to live at 1,600m (5,250ft) for three months. Walking on the steep, stoney ground makes the horses hardy and strong. At the age of three and a half they are sent for training before appearing at the Riding School.

Further east is the fertile plain of the river Danube, on which the capital, Vienna, stands. A fifth of the seven and a half million inhabitants of Austria live in the capital.

Fourth in Europe

Austria is comparatively poor in raw materials. It has only a little coal, some iron ore, petroleum and timber. Eighty per cent of its coal is imported from Poland and over half its gas requirements from Russia. Hydro-electric schemes in the Tyrol are important sources of power for the industrial areas around Linz, Graz and Vienna.

Iron and steelmaking are major industries. The oxygen lance method of steelmaking, which revolutionised the speed at which steel could be made, was pioneered by an Austrian inventor, Voest, in Linz.

Tourism is a vital source of income for Austria. It comprises about eight per cent of the annual national income. Over half the tourists in Austria come from Germany with which it shares a common border and language.

Money matters

The unit of currency in Austria is the **schilling.** Find out how many schilling there are to the pound sterling when you are in Austria. You will come across notes worth 20, 100, 500 and even 1,000 schillings. There are 100 **groschen** to the schilling and coins are in units of 1, 2, 10 and 50 groschen.

Things to do

1. The composers Haydn, Mozart, Schubert, Brahms and Strauss all lived and worked in Vienna.
   a) Match each composer in the list below to one of his most famous works:

Strauss	Trout Quintet
Mozart	Blue Danube
Haydn	Eine Kleine Nachtmusik
Schubert	Surprise Symphony

2. Match each of the following with the town or city with which it is associated:

Spanish Riding School	Linz
First ski school	St Anton
The Sound of Music	Salzburg
Oxygen lance steel	Vienna

3. Like Switzerland, Austria now has a policy of neutrality. How do you think this might affect Austria's relations with the following:
   The UN; The EEC; NATO; The USSR?

Austrians on the road

The first letter on each car number plate indicates the region or town of origin. For example, W stands for Wien (German for Vienna) and S stands for Salzburg.

Austrian food

Viennese pastries are famous all over the world. They are filled with fruit and usually served with generous helpings of whipped cream. Apfelstrudel is an apple-filled pastry topped with nuts.

Speaking the language

Here are a few basic phrases you may like to try. To help with the pronunciation, *ie* is said as *ee* and *ei* is said as a capital *I* in English.

Good day – *Guten Tag*
Goodbye – *Auf Wiedersehn*
Please – *Bitte*
Thank you – *Danke*
Sorry – *Sorry* (the same!)
Don't mention it – *Bitte*
Where is? – *Wo ist?*
The toilet – *Die Toilette*
A telephone – *Ein Telefon*
Do you speak English? – *Sprechen Sie Englisch?*
Yes – *Ja*
No – *Nein*

Index

You and your group

Name..

School..

Resort..

Hotel..

Dates of tour..

Best moment of tour..

....

....

....

....

....

....

....

....

....

....

....

Use the space on the opposite page to:
a) Collect the autographs of everyone in your group (including teachers)
b) Stick in a postcard or photograph of your resort and/or hotel.
c) Attach a photograph or colour a picture of the national flag.